# Doc Zoo Combat Medic

Robert W. Costigan & Helen A. Cummings

*Sheepcote Publishing*
*Copyright © 2005 Robert W. Costigan and*
*Helen A. Cummings*
*All Rights Reserved*
Printed in U. S. A.

*AuthorHouse™*
*1663 Liberty Drive, Suite 200*
*Bloomington, IN 47403*
*www.authorhouse.com*
*Phone: 1-800-839-8640*

*© 2007 Robert W. Costigan & Helen A. Cummings. All rights reserved.*

*No part of this book may be reproduced, stored in*
*a retrieval system, or transmitted by any means*
*without the written permission of the author.*

*First published by AuthorHouse 12/16/2007*

*ISBN: 978-1-4343-3100-7 (sc)*

*Library of Congress Control Number: 2007905701*

*Printed in the United States of America*
*Bloomington, Indiana*

*This book is printed on acid-free paper.*
On the Cover From Left to Right
  Medivac Helicopter
  Map of Vietnam
  Jump Wings
  173rd Airborne Brigade Patch
  Combat Medic's Badge

Original Cover Art by Gerald Rolf
Original Illustrations by Chris Cummings

To all the men who served with me, I would like to sincerely thank you. Thank you for always being there for me under the worst circumstances that any human being should have to endure. You are the bravest and toughest that the Elite could offer. You are men who would rather face death than surrender. You were in my thoughts then, now and into eternity. AIRBORNE ALL THE WAY (THE HERD).

# Introduction
## 173rd Airborne Brigade (Sep.) History

On March 26, 1963, the Army activated the 173rd Airborne Brigade on the island of Okinawa. From it's beginning, it proved to be an aggressive and unique unit led by (then) Brigadier General Ellis W. Williamson. The 173rd Brigade is an all-volunteer unit. The General established realistic training throughout the Pacific Region.

The "Sky Soldiers", as the Nationalist Chinese paratroopers called the 173rd, made thousands of parachute jumps in a dozen different Pacific area countries. They were known as the "Fire Brigade" on Okinawa. That is because the Army could drop the 173rd in any of the Southeast Asian countries as needed.

The unit was an elite group of soldiers. To call Reveille, the Battalion Commander erected a number of very large speakers, which blasted the song "Rawhide" all over the camp.

Every morning the blaring words "head 'em up, move 'em out, Rawhide" or something to that effect rousted Sky Soldiers from their bunks. This is why the entire 173rd Airborne Brigade's nickname became "The Herd".

The Brigade was the first Army Unit sent to the Republic of South Vietnam. During more than six years of nearly continuous combat in Vietnam, the Brigade earned 14 campaign streamers and 4 unit citations, 13 Medal of Honor recipients, 137 Distinguished Service Cross recipients, more than 6,000 Purple Hearts and the only Combat Parachute Assault of the War. Sadly, the Vietnam Memorial Wall has 1,700 names of 173rd soldiers inscribed on its face.

The Army deactivated the Brigade on January 14, 1972 at Fort Campbell, Kentucky and then reactivated it in Vicenza, Italy on June 6, 2000. On March 26, 2003, the 173rd Airborne Brigade again became the only airborne unit to perform a combat jump when it parachuted into Northern Iraq to the Northern front of Operation Iraqi Freedom. (173rd Airborne Brigade Archives and 173rd Airborne Brigade, In Country Brochure).

# A Trip Into The Unknown

## January 1969

---

  I was relatively new in country (to Vietnam). After serving a brief stay with the Fifth Special Forces Group, I transferred to the famous 173rd Airborne Brigade, stationed in the Central Highlands of Vietnam. I would work as a Medic.

  A Helicopter transported me to a place called LZ Uplift. It was a fire support base just north of the Crescent Valley. (LZ or Landing Zone is usually a small clearing secured temporarily for the landing of re-supply Helicopters. Some Landing Zones become more permanent and eventually become base camps).

  I had a free day or two. I checked out the Aid Station and wrote letters to home while I waited for my assignment in my roll as a Medic. It was a challenge to get myself acclimated to this very new and weird place.

At first, I felt like a stranger but I quickly made a few friends. One early afternoon, I was sitting outside at my makeshift sleeping quarters. Two very nasty, raggedy ass looking Paratroopers walked up to me and asked me my name and what Company I was with.

*Doc Zoo cleans blood from a Medevac Helicopter at CO B Medical, LZ Uplift.*

*I told them that I just came from a Special Forces assignment. My new station was with Headquarters Company/Company B Medical working as a Dustoff (Medevac) Medic and helping in the Aid Station. At least they agreed that my being a Medic was a good thing. As if by mutual agreement between them, they said something like, "That's cool, man, he's a Medic".*

They introduced themselves and started joking about me being a Cherry. It seemed that they made a private decision between them because one of the Sky Soldiers said to me, "Okay, Doc, how would you like to go with us tonight on a little adventure, down to Bong Song?"

*A well to do Vietnamese family of farmers in Bong Song.*

I admit I was skeptical, so I rather hesitated for a moment before I asked them, "What are we going to do there?"

The reply was, "We're going to party". It was hotter than shit at LZ Uplift and visions of drinking some beer got my attention. I agreed to go.

They said, "Okay, we'll be back for you come sun down. Make sure you're armed."

*Zoo works out with homemade barbells he fashioned from concrete while at LZ Uplift.*

Little did I know we were breaking Army Regulations by leaving the Landing Zone. Their warning to make sure I was armed made me feel even more hesitant and unsettled. The Paratroopers assured me,

"Don't worry about it man, we got you covered. We're going to have some fun in Bong Song and we'll be back before any one even knows we're gone."

By now, I had a strong feeling that this was the wrong thing to do, but the two Sky Soldiers befriended me. I figured, "What the hell, I'll go".

It was a little past dark when five Paratroopers arrived at my quarters, including the two that I previously met. I heard one of the Paratroopers say, "Go get the Cherry and let's get going." (Cherry was slang for a soldier who has never been under fire).

There was a small hole in a fence line, constructed of barbed wire. It ran behind a bunker. Outside this line ran three more fence lines of barbed wire, all strung up with a variety of tin cans. If someone challenged the perimeter, the noise from the cans would alert the soldier with the Fifty Caliber Machine Gun, guarding the bunker. He was always ready to shoot at anything that made those tin cans rattle.

The Paratroopers led the way through the barbed wire. It was so sharp that it threatened to cut us all to ribbons before we made it through the hazard. We had to slowly negotiate around and between the rows of thorny, barbed wire without setting off any of the Claymore Mines planted between the rows.

I thought to myself. "Here's our guys trying to keep the NVA/VC out and we are trying to leave and maybe blow ourselves up at the same time."

We finally arrived on the other side of the barbed wire barrier. So away, we go into the semi darkness of a secondary (not a thick) jungle. The farther we moved away from the LZ, the more nervous I became. I felt increasingly like a Cherry. I worried that I might be doing something and going somewhere that is off limits.

After about forty minutes, we stepped out of the jungle near the back door of a hut, in a place called Bong Song. One of the Paratroopers knocked on the back door of the Vietnamese dwelling.

A mamason readily welcomed us in. I figured this was not the first visit here for the soldiers that invited me on this adventure.

The House Proprietress or mamason, which is the more familiar address, treated us to beer and soda that was somewhat cool. Her daughters, as well as some other people, who also lived in the house, were present.

Someone turned on a small cassette player. I could not believe the song coming out of the tinny sounding speaker. It was "In-A-Gadda-Da-Vida". This was almost like a holy experience to hear a song by Iron Butterfly here in the middle of a jungle, in some native hut with these strange people.

*Mamason carries food to sell at the market in Bong Song.*

*I sat in somewhat ease and contentment and sipped on a warm beer. Then I smelled something funny. I did not know that in a few more minutes I was going to get high for the first time in my life.*

*The Paratroopers told me the smell was "grass". "Grass", I thought to myself. "Who in their fucking right mind would want to smoke the grass off the ground when you have a good cigarette sitting in your pocket?" I was so naive that I thought their "grass" was what I pictured in my mind; grass on a lawn! Time passed and soon a pipe arrived. One of the Paratroopers told me to just take easy hits. At first, I thought it was tobacco. Well, maybe it is Vietnamese tobacco.*

*After the pipe came to me a few more times, I found myself sitting motionless and staring at a candle, on a table, in the middle of the room. I was really enjoying the music and thought to myself.*

*"This ain't too bad. If Nam is going to be like this, I'm going to have a lot of fun". I felt good, even though I could not understand why my legs felt like they weighed about five hundred pounds each and that I still felt paralyzed.*

*We enjoyed ourselves as the music played and the pipe went around. We kept our voices low when we talked, not forgetting that we were in enemy territory. A shroud of curtains hung across the doorway to the main living room where we sat.*

*Suddenly, the mamason came swiftly through the doorway with a deep concern and tremendous fear on her face. She kept saying, in a low, urgent voice. "Yap de, yap de!" That meant, "Shut up".*

*She pointed toward the front of the building and whispered, "Beaucoup (many) NVA outside door". Then she urged in English, "You must shut up and go."*

*It seems that a Company of NVA Regulars who just perpetrated a mortar attack on Phu Cat Air Force Base were on their way to the whorehouses to hide out. Unfortunately, they decided to entertain themselves right at the place where we were partying. Note: LZ Uplift is twelve miles South of Bong Song. Phu Cat and Bong Song are thirty miles apart.*

We experienced an immediate adrenalin rush that kicked into high as we all came to the realization, at the same time, that we were in deep shit. Fear reared its head among us, in the small room. We did not move or make a sound. We stared at the door, with fingers to our lips as a warning to be silent. We were not sure how many of the enemy was outside, but we were damn, sure concerned.

Then, one of the Paratroopers whispered, "I'll be right back". He went out the back door and around the corner of the building to check out the opposition. After a minute or so of observation, he arrived at the back door of the mamason's hut again.

He announced in a hushed voice. "Well, gentlemen, we are really fucked now!" He was not lying. He went on to explain that there were about one hundred heavily armed North Vietnamese Soldiers at mamason's front door.

As me and the other Sky Soldiers digested this information, there was a sudden knock on the door. The mamason slowly moved towards the door. She nervously looked back at us. We moved away from the doorway, out of sight.

The mamason opened the door to a North Vietnamese Officer who had a gun in his hand. He was checking her out while she answered his questions. As the mamason assured the Officer that she and her girls were having a peaceful evening at home, our intense situation in the back room became almost unbearable.

We were steeling ourselves for the reality of a possible conflict. The tension in the room mounted. I gently pushed my finger down on the selector switch of my M-16 and got ready to rock'n'roll (firing a weapon on full automatic).

Joe, one of the Paratroopers, began motioning me to move to my right by signaling with his eyes. He motioned the other soldiers to move to their left then he sat down on the floor and produced a LAW rocket from his stash of weapons. (A shoulder-fired, 66-millimeter rocket. The launcher is made of Fiberglass, and is disposable after one shot).

Joe quickly armed the rocket. He was facing the shrouded curtain, which led to the front door. He had his eye on the sight and everybody quickly moved to avoid the back blast from the propulsion of the rocket.

It was sinking into my head fast that there was going to be one hell of a gunfight. I thought to myself. "Swell! We are five against an army".

The Vietnamese Officer at the door did not have a clue that five enemy soldiers were hiding in mamason's back room. Furthermore, we were fully armed and ready to get as many of their Army as we could, if a fight broke out. The intensity level was now beyond anything I ever felt before. I do believe I went beyond petrified and back. I also came back with a bad attitude and ready to fight.

The five minutes that this exercise in terror lasted seemed more like hours. The Vietnamese Officer at the door finally seemed satisfied with his observation of mamason's hut. He bid them a good evening.

We were already on our way out the back door as the mamason was closing her front door to the Vietnamese Officer.

We figured it had to be a miracle that the Vietnamese Army did not spot us leaving. As we fled back through the jungle, I swore I would never do such a stupid thing again. My legs were still under the influence of the Marijuana and I had a hell of a time walking, much less running back to the LZ. It felt like someone filled my boots with concrete before we left the mamason's house in Bong Song.

We finally got back to the LZ. I said to one of the Sky Soldiers, "If there's that many NVA in that village, they might attack this LZ tonight".

I went and told a Bn Staff Duty Officer that we spotted some heavy movement along the perimeter line. It looked like the North Vietnamese Army was moving towards our position.

This was truly speculation, on my part. But by telling the Bn Staff Duty Officer about the NVA close by, it was a good way to cover up where we really were if word got back to Command about our little trip.

Everything was quiet in the camp for most of the evening. I felt great relief as I lay on my cot. I said to myself, "You were lucky this time. Don't do that again".

*The Central Highlands, pictured above is where Bong Song is located. Ho Chi Minh Trail or Highway 1 is in the background.*

I could not stop thinking about the near run in with the NVA. About ten minutes later, our LZ was under a mortar fire attack by the enemy. A quick response from our camp sent a mortar attack right back on the enemy's location.

All hell broke loose for about ten minutes. Then it was suddenly quiet again. I really think the enemy had a different agenda other than us. They were just passing through and buzzing our position.

Our adventure in the village was like going to Disneyland in a snowstorm. Lucky for us, we managed to keep the story about our almost confrontation with the North Vietnamese Army from getting back to Command. Because of our devious adventure, we were able to alert our LZ Command that the NVA, with heavy firepower, was in the area and possibly heading our way.

Our misadventure that evening ended up saving many lives because we gave the alert and the 1st Bn/503 Infantry and the 3rd Bn/503 Infantry or Herds were waiting!

Note: a Company was composed of 3 Rifle Platoons, one Mortar Platoon, 3 Rifle Squads, 1 FDC Section and 3 Mortar Squads and 2 Fire Teams.

# Amazing Brace

Medcaps, used as a public relations tool, allowed a Medic to go into certain Vietnamese villages, in different locations. The Medic administered first aid treatment to the general population of the village. I participated in several of these Medcaps with the Special Forces and assisted the Doctor with medical treatment.

The villagers ranged in age from small children to adults and possibly the NVA and Viet Cong without us even knowing it. The effort was to help the sick and needy and to keep them away from normal military operations and off any secured LZs or secured military installations. A Medcap usually lasted most of the day because it was one large sick call. During the course of the day, you might treat and see up to eighty or more people.

Ailments ranged from a minor cut to a situation requiring stitches. I also rendered medical care to pregnant women, treated children, and adults. I always tried to take time to educate my patients a little in the art of preventive medicine.

Most of the time when I was doing such a task, either Republic of Vietnam Soldiers or a Platoon of Infantrymen would accompany me from the 173rd.

This particular day a Senior Medical NCO asked if I would go down to Tam Mi, a village close to LZ Uplift, and check on a couple of little children that had some kind of infection.

Zoo and a RVN soldier stands near his Jeep. Zoo often took Republic of Vietnam Soldiers on Medcaps when no U.S. Troops were available because they were in the field.

I found out that there were no Republic of Vietnam Soldiers for me to take as security that day. Most of the soldiers from the 173$^{rd}$ were in the jungle, so that eliminated them as bodyguards, also. I wondered if the Medical NCO would cancel the Medcap.

At first, I volunteered to go by myself because it was a relatively safe area. There were no circumstances (Army Regulations) however, that would allow me to go without some sort of an armed escort.

As I packed the Jeep with various medical supplies, the Senior NCO tried to locate someone to go with me for security. I came out of the Aid Station with a big box full of bandages and noticed four MPs (Military Police) escorting a rather large, well-groomed black soldier. The handcuffs and shackles at his ankles told a tale. Escape was not an option for him. The MPs walked him right towards the
Aid Station. As they went past me, I noticed that the captive soldier appeared to have a very bad attitude towards life.

I placed the bandages in the jeep and returned to the Aid Station to see what the problem was with the handcuffed soldier. I walked up towards the Soldier, who was sitting on one of the litters, and noticed that his neck was bleeding. The MPs were not making life any easier for this disgruntled Soldier. They warned me to approach the man with extreme caution, as he was very dangerous.

I said to one of the MPs, "I have to look at his neck. Can we get his shirt off him?"

They would not take the handcuffs off the Soldier, even though they were armed. I wanted to ask what this man did to get himself into this predicament, because in all the time I was in the military I never saw a soldier in hand cuffs and shackles in a war zone.

I assured the Soldier I did not intend to hurt him. I just wanted to treat his wound. He was reluctant for me to touch him, at first. Once he realized I meant no harm, however, he let me examine his neck. He had a small puncture that required several stitches. I sewed him up and told him he was good to go.

Just then, the Senior NCO came back and said, "I don't know, Zoo, I can't find anyone to go with you to the village".

I said, "What about him?" as I pointed to the soldier I just stitched up. "His size would make King Kong blush".

My Senior NCO thought for a second, and then agreed to let the big man go with me. He made it very clear and that I was responsible for him. The MPs were very reluctant to unshackle the soldier, because they believed that he wanted to break every bone in their bodies.

After finally persuading the guards to remove the prisoner's shackles, the soldier got in the jeep with me. He seemed very reluctant about doing anything or going anywhere with me. I told him, "This beats being in shackles".

He was unarmed at that point, but no one knew that I had extra weapons hidden under the medical supplies. We got to the gate I explained to the MP guards that I was just going to a village that was that was right outside the LZ. I told them that if they hear any shots fired to come and get us.

After we cleared the gate, I handed the soldier a loaded M-16 Rifle, a bandolier of ammunition and a couple hand grenades. I told him that when we got to the village I wanted him to secure the Northern part while I did my medical work.

We proceeded to the village. Because I did not know how this soldier would act, I asked him not to run away on me, or do anything that will end up in my court martial. I was really depending on this man for a backup. I told him, "Don't do anything stupid like running away and I will talk to someone when we got back about your predicament".

*A young boy asked Zoo if he could hold his gun. The boy is from one of the Villages outside of LZ Uplift where Zoo administered Medcaps.*

I did not think the soldier did anything that serious, or they would not have let him out of the irons.

Perhaps they put him in restraints until he could calm down.

When I got to the village, I set up a portable medical aid station on the Jeep. It did not take long for the villagers to realize that I was a Medic because of the Red Cross on the side of the vehicle. Soon, there was a line of people stretching through half the place, including babies, young and older children, and adults.

They knew about the new program called "Peace and Pacification" through leaflets that were dropped from airplanes. They knew medical assistance was available and that they would get hygiene supplies.

This was the first Medcap that I ever attempted by myself. I had full confidence in what I was doing, even as my mind kept thinking of my freshly unleashed partner. I looked to see where the big soldier was. He had himself stationed where I asked him to go. As the morning grew into early afternoon, the heat and humidity became oppressive. Six people still stood in line when I noticed a large crowd of young children gathering. They discovered that I brought candy with me.

I told them that they would only get candy when I was finished attending to the medical needs of the remainder of the people in line. They did not want to wait, but they did.

I just finished with the last patient when suddenly little children started surrounding the Jeep and me. They reminded me of a shark feeding frenzy. I conveyed to one of the village leaders, that if he did not stop the kids from mauling me I would go back to the LZ with the candy and eat it myself.

He told this to the eagerly waiting children, who finally stopped grabbing my clothes and in general battering me.

I put away the remainder of the medical supplies in the Jeep, and then called for Brace to come back from his guard duty at the end of the village. I needed him to help me pass out the stuff to the kids.

I took a long gulp of warm water from my canteen before I opened a large box of candy, soap and assorted items that the Senior NCO had put in the Jeep. I did not realize how much was in there until I started handing out the stuff. The children and their parents pressed in upon Brace and me, grabbing for any thing they could get their hands on. It was soon becoming a scary free for all.

Finally, Brace and I picked up the whole box and tossed the contents in the air. Everybody dived for the stuff, which took the pressure off us. I kept my hand on my forty-five and told Brace to hold onto his M-16. These people wanted to take everything we had. It seemed everyone in the village was happy to see us arrive and sad to see us go. They asked how long it would be until we returned. I had no idea when our next visit would be, so we just conveyed to them that we would be back as soon as possible.

On the ride back to the LZ, Brace said to me, "You know I think I was safer in handcuffs and shackles than back there with that mob of kids". He also said he had a pretty neat day helping me out and that if I ever wanted him to come with me again, he would be willing to help with security.

*Medcap – Doc Zoo, in rear, giving candy to village children.*

I asked him how he got into the predicament with the handcuffs and shackles. He just shook his head and became silent. The very second that we returned to Company B Medical, we were met by MPs who took Brace back into custody and led him away from the Aid Station.

To this day, I only knew him by Brace. I had no idea why he was in shackles. However, I would sure not want to be the enemy confronted by him. I never saw him again after that.

From then on, I pulled several Medcaps in the same village, called Tam Mi with some members of the 1st/ 503rd Airborne Infantry. I was happy to have these men with me during the Medcaps, as security. It was easier to do my job when I did not have to worry about someone killing me.

The village of Tam Mi was located about one thousand meters North of LZ Uplift. On the West side of the Village was located the 506 Valley. To the

North of that was the Crescent Valley. The NVA/Viet Cong operated in and around these areas. I pulled several more Medcaps. After a few months I had the occupants in the Villages I visited, pretty well healed from parasites, rashes, diseases, shrapnel wounds and other assorted ailments.

It was a bad situation for the Villagers. When the NVA came into the area, they would look for clues that the Americans were there before them. If they found a cigarette butt or a candy wrapper, they would punish the people living there for allowing Americans into their Village.

Cigarette burns on children and broken bones for Mom and Dad were just some of the things the NVA/Viet Cong gave to the people of these small Villages. They tortured the people in retaliation for the "Peace and Pacification" Program that the United States sponsored.

# Transition

## February 1969

---

After several months of working at Company B's Medical Aid Station at LZ Uplift, I got the proper training that I needed from the Medical Staff on hand. My skills became sharper and my knowledge of medicine grew as the days went on.

Company B Medical had a facility, similar to a small hospital, but not as large as a MASH Unit. They had me assisting with amputations, gunshot wounds, delivering babies, and working in the Brigade Pharmacy. My love for medicine grew stronger. It made me feel good to help others get through all the pain and suffering that they arrived with, at the Aid Station. We treated all patients, including wounded soldiers from the field and civilians, men, women, and children.

At that point, in my young career, it seemed that the Doctors, Surgeons, and Senior Medical NCOs were pleased and satisfied with my performance at CO B Medical Aid Station. As the intriguing sign at the entrance to the Aid Station points out, this was definitely a war zone.

*Sign outside CO B Medical Aid Station, LZ Uplift near Bong Song, Vietnam.*

Sometimes in my spare moments, I hung around the small radio shack. It was located near the Aid Station. I listened to what was going on in the field. It was always easy to eavesdrop on what was happening in the jungles and we would get first hand knowledge about casualties on their way to the Aid Station via Dustoff Medevac.

It was a little past Midnight, and raining hard. I could not sleep. I got up and started walking around in the pouring rain. I lit a cigarette and walked over to the Aid Station. It was manned twenty-four hours a day. One of my friends was busily cleaning up around the area where the wounded are treated. I asked him, "What's happening?"

He said, "Not much. It's pretty quiet out there because it's raining hard".

*Co B Medical, Doc Zoo takes break from Aid Station.*

We talked for about a half hour about home and what we were going to do when we got back to "the world".

I was tired and decided to go back to bed. I was asleep about an hour when the noise of the Medevac Helicopter cranking up awoke me. It was about sixty feet from my small makeshift hut of sandbags and metal tin roof. Soon, a knock came on the door of my hooch and a voice yelled,

"You gotta get up, we have wounded coming in about ten to fifteen minutes. Hurry up and get over to the Aid Station".

*Dustoff (Medevac) Helicopter, CO B Medical, LZ Uplift*

The seriousness of the injuries or the number of incoming wounded was unknown at that moment. I got dressed and was on my way to the Aid Station.

The rain grew more intense. It was almost impossible to see in front of me. I wondered how the Helicopter Pilots could fly in this kind of weather, when you could not even see the ground.

I got into the Aid Station. The full staff of Doctors and Medics was there and ready to take care of the wounded. The Medevac Helicopters already radioed that they had ten wounded on the way back to the Aid Station: both Republic of Vietnam and Americans.

The rain slowed a little. From the distance, I could hear the Helicopters coming towards our location. They landed on the Helipad directly outside the Aid Station. There were two Medevac Helicopters and one Gun ship all loaded down with wounded.

Everybody at the Aid Station ran to the Helicopters and tried to get the wounded out of the rain. It was especially difficult to carry the wounded from the Gun ship, as they were not equipped with stretchers.

Accommodations at the Aid Station included, a makeshift surgical unit, which had the ability to take care of eight wounded soldiers. If there was more than eight at a time, space was at a premium. Some patients were on stretchers on the floor, for lack of any other place to put them.

This night, that started out so quiet, became endless. We got the wounded that just arrived stabilized and ready to go to a larger facility for additional medical treatment.

Then, a call came into the Aid Station that there were six more wounded coming in from a jungle battle. We began wondering where we could put the newly arriving wounded soldiers because we ran out of space.

The non-stop action in the field kept us up for the rest of the night. Wounded arrived at the Aid Station all through the hours of darkness, in groups of three, five and sometimes seven.

Again, because the Aid Station could only accommodate up to eight wounded, we sometimes had patients outside the Station in the dirt on stretchers. The activity went on all night long. Our medical supplies began to run low and everyone was exhausted. One of the Senior NCOs radioed to another Aid Station in the area. He cited the emergency and requested medical supplies for the LZ Uplift Aid Station as soon as possible.

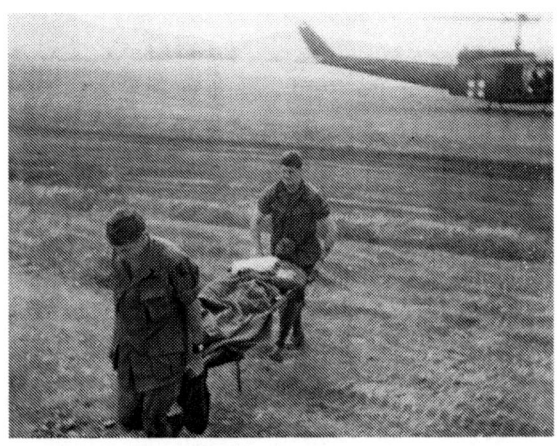

*Medic, Bob Costigan (rear) helps carry wounded Medic from the Dustoff Helicopter after a hard fight with the Viet Cong somewhere in the Central Highlands.*

I felt that we might be in for an equally long day as the horrible night had been. It was a little after six in the morning. Another Dustoff (Medevac) coming in radioed that they had two wounded aboard, including the Dustoff Medic.

As we waited, we saw the Dustoff (Medevac) in the distance. It appeared the Aircraft was in trouble because it trailed smoke from the engine compartment as it neared the landing sight.

The bird careened through the air in a crazy pattern while the Pilot desperately tried to make it to the landing pad. The Helicopter finally landed, and everyone scrambled to the Aircraft to retrieve the wounded. The wounded Dustoff Medic was on the stretcher that I helped carry to the Aid Station.

He seemed lifeless, with his head tilted to his left side. Blood was pouring down his face from under the face shield of his helmet. I yelled to the person carrying the other end of the stretcher, "Hurry up, I think he's going to die on us".

When we got him inside the Aid Station, most of the Doctors and NCOs were busily working on other patients. I said to another Medic,

"Let's put him down over here in the corner fast".

The Dustoff Medic had a traumatic head injury. In the process of stabilizing him, I began an intravenous line. I was trying to stop the bleeding in his head with direct pressure as I called to the Surgeon,

"Please come over here, and help me out when you get a chance".

The Surgeon yelled back to me. "I'll be there in a second",

I continued direct pressure on the head wound. The Surgeon finally came to my side. I showed him the head wound. The Surgeon examined the patient and saw that the back of his skull was missing. I could not feel a pulse and the Surgeon pronounced the Medic dead.

Another Doctor came over. He cried, "Oh fuck" and began mourning the loss of one of the best Medics in the Army. Two new Medics, at the Aid Station, wore stunned looks on their faces as they put their fallen comrade in a body bag and filled out the necessary paperwork.

As they zipped the body bag up, I became sick to my stomach from the smell of the dried blood. I ran outside and got some fresh air. I thought to myself that the little trip I had earlier taken to Bong Song when I was new in country was nothing compared to the death of this Medic.

From that time on, death became a familiar companion. I knew I was getting hardened to war. The death of that Medic placed me right into the reality of war.

I promised myself right then that I would keep as many of my friends alive as I possibly could. I did not know at the time that I was about to take the place of the fallen Dustoff Medic.

# The Call Of The Wild

They say that all forms of life adapt to their surroundings, for example, insects, fish, animals, and birds. For me, I adapted to the Tiger Mountain's jungles.

After months, with no end, of listening to all kinds of jungle sounds from Macaws, Elephants, Tigers and primates, I started to imitate the sounds of the wildlife. I did it almost to perfection.

One night at LZ Uplift, a small gathering at a bunker, occupied by an all Black Male cast of soldiers, invited me out to spend some time with them.

They asked me if I was Doc Zoo, the guy that made the animal sounds. I replied, "Yea, that's me". One brother stood up. His name was Willy from Philly. He said to the other soldiers, "No shit check this guy out.

He sounds like the perfect deal. Wait until you hear his Tiger calls". After I made several animal noises, I had them laughing. One soldier looked at me and said, "Shit Zoo, you're the whole fucking jungle, man".

Pretty soon I had people (including officers) from all over the 173rd Airborne coming to see me for various health reasons and for me to make a jungle call of some sort. The soldiers had their favorite animal sounds.

Before I enlisted in the Army, I had a lot of experience in practicing the Martial Arts. I was able to keep up on my karate practice thanks to two young men in a nearby village outside of LZ Uplift who acted as my instructors.

*Zoo's karate instructors in a Village outside of LZ Uplift.*

One night while I was alone, I was reading a manual on Psychological Warfare, and decided to use some of my Special Forces talents and make my own Psychological plan. I took into consideration how the NVA/Viet Cong used Psychological Warfare on Americans.

The jungle was very quiet at night. There were no jungle sounds to hear. I sometimes threw large rocks out into the vegetation. They ricocheted off the trees and sounded like a herd of Elephants trampling through the dense jungle undergrowth. The noise would wake the monkeys and every other animal in the rain forest.

At every opportunity, I used jungle sounds, especially the Tiger, to mess with the enemy's head. The big cat's growl was a very useful instrument for intimidating the NVA.

I would go out in the jungle at night with a cardboard roll. I would start with some subtle Tiger growls. Soon I would hear the NVA saying to each other, "Tiger! Tiger!" After some more aggressive growls, they would move to another position for fear of the Tiger they thought was stalking them in the jungle.

The nickname of "Zoo" stuck through my three tours of duty in Vietnam. To this day, all of the soldiers I served with still call me Zoo.

# Transportation

The most feasible means of transportation during the Vietnam War was not a backbreaking hike through the jungle or a brisk hike up a mountain. This type of hike would leave a mountain goat laboring for breath from sheer exhaustion. The main transportation during the Vietnam War became the Helicopter.

There were no fronts of war in the Vietnam conflict, where opposing armies engaged and advanced. The object being to hold the ground they covered.

Instead, the Helicopter allowed the U.S. to quickly carry troops into a hostile area and deploy them with some element of surprise.

The Army then removed the troops to a new location, after the fighting ended. While there was no ground held because of this tactic, it often proved to be successful. Aviation was the best means to relocate and deploy ground troops from one point to another almost instantaneously. The average soldier in Vietnam experienced three times as much combat as soldiers in WW II due to the use of Helicopter transportation.

The most versatile Helicopter used in Vietnam was the Huey. This Helicopter had three personalities. It flew as a Dustoff (Medevac) when the Army used it to extract wounded from the field. When retrofitted as a Medevac aircraft, the Huey UH-1 Utility Helicopter or Slick could carry six or seven infantrymen with full gear or seven litters of wounded.

The Huey UH-1 Utility Helicopter also served as a Hog or a Gun ship. Mini Guns (7.62 MM) and rockets were its main ammo. The versatile aircraft transported men to and from the field. It became the main means of transportation for the infantry soldier in Vietnam. Command could move a Company from one location to another quickly.

The even more sophisticated, Huey Assault Helicopter, armed with Gatling Guns and rockets, transported men to the field, and provided backup firepower for troops under fire. There was a large number of Hueys left in the RVN after the war.

*An Loa Valley, the heart of the Viet Cong.
Photo taken from a Medevac Chopper.*

The Army also used spotter planes. These fixed wing aircraft, flew high over the jungle. They employed sophisticated camera equipment to track enemy movements. The planes could also visually locate the enemy.

The OH, a small light observation Helicopter such as the OH-6-Cayuse, performed reconnaissance missions. Two soldiers usually manned it. The OH was highly maneuverable.

One time in the jungle, we played cat and mouse with the NVA for half a day. We originally saw four of them. We tracked them, then lost them. Our Point Man spotted them again. We tried to take a shortcut to head them off and lost them again. Lieutenant Ed called in our position.

*A Huey retrofitted for Medevac missions going out to pick up wounded from LZ English.*

We awaited further instructions on what to do when suddenly, an OH-6 appeared from nowhere. It buzzed the jungle like a gnat. We felt surprise as we saw the thing flit from place to place. We never saw an aircraft like this in combat before. The OH dropped green smoke grenades down on the enemy's position, taking enemy fire as it did so. Then all of a sudden, it disappeared. We all wondered where the hell it went.

The OH Birds carried only one mini gun (because of the weight of ammo it used). The Pilot and Observer also had a M60 machine gun, and a M79 grenade launcher. To complete the armament the Bird also had on board frags (fragmentation grenades) and white phosphorus.

The gnat suddenly appeared in the sky again. He was not alone. He returned to our position with a small swarm of his friends. The noise filled the air like a model airplane convention. My Platoon had to get to a safer area, yet Command told us to maintain our position.

We were still wondering what was going on when an OH, armed with a Gatling gun on the right side, appeared above us.

Then a Cobra Gun ship entered the fray. The two Helicopters proceeded to fire near the green smoke. In less than a minute, the OH cut down the trees.

Then the Cobra and the OH were side by side. The Cobra moved to the right of the OH and banked at a 45-degree angle.

*A Cobra near LZ English waiting for F-4 Jet to stop bombing Viet Cong so we can get in to pick up six wounded GI's and one KIA. February 12, 1969.*

The two Helicopters fired together in a V form, and destroyed the enemy and everything else in their paths. They used rockets and 7.62-millimeter Gatling guns.

The Cobra and the OH then disappeared. The gnat stayed to assess the damage to the enemy. When he lifted his sunshade on his helmet, I could see he had a mustache. He saluted our Platoon then flew quickly backwards, turned around and disappeared. I asked the Lieutenant, "What the fuck was that?"

He replied, "It is a new type of Helicopter designed just for our war". As we held our positions, they made short work of what could have been a deadly situation for my Platoon.

The Hueys used for troop transportation came armed with M60 machine guns (one on each side). In addition, a door gunner used a mounted 7.62MM M60 machine gun to keep the enemy at bay while loading wounded.

While deploying troops, the Helicopter hovered above waist high elephant grass as landing infantry soldiers jumped from the aircraft.

The razor sharp herbage made the soldier's lives even more miserable than it already was because they often endured getting cut by the stuff as they excited the Helicopter.

In a Hot LZ, the Helicopters would come in five feet from the ground and the soldiers had to jump off with a full rucksack. All the while, the Pilot usually could be heard shouting, "Get off my fucking Helicopter!"

This was just another asshole, fucking thing to endure. It caused many injuries to Soldier's knees and ankles. I used to call this the "Jump for your life".

My heavy rucksack added enough weight to my landing that I often found myself buried in the swamps. I finally learned that when we were going to be jumping out of a Helicopter, I took my rucksack off and threw it out first. I jumped off with only my rifle or shotgun and then would grab my rucksack after I landed. I always made sure that my hand grenades had extra tape around the spoons so they would not explode when my rucksack hit the ground.

Another means of deployment into the jungle, seldom used but I thought was a much better method, was the CH 47 Chinook Helicopter. It could easily hold over forty infantrymen and their equipment. The nice thing about the Chinook is that it had a ramp in the rear that you walked down to exit the aircraft, instead of jumping into swamps. However, the original intent was to use the aircraft for cargo and that was how it was mostly deployed.

The best thing about riding to and from the jungle in a Helicopter was that I finally got a breeze through the open door. On the ground, it seemed like God took all the air away.

# First Flight As A Dustoff (Medevac) Medic

The thought of the dead Medic still deeply embedded itself in my heart and mind. There was sadness around the Aid Station. He was remembered as conscientious and a very good Medic. We would miss him.

I just returned to my hut after cleaning up the Aid Station. A Senior Medical NCO approached me. He asked me if I would like to try flying Dustoff (Medevac) for a few missions, to see how I liked it. As soon as he said that, I knew this would not be a try out, but a permanent assignment.

I assured him that I was very eager to take the place of the deceased Medic and that I would do the best that I possibly could.

I knew in my heart that I was going to be okay. The medicine I learned at the Aid Station, gave me enough knowledge to be able to treat and stabilize the wounded as the Medevac Helicopter returned from the jungle.

I went out on my first Medevac Mission the next day, after being fitted with a flight suit and helmet. The request came in for a Dustoff (Medevac) a little after lunch. I can still remember my lunch that day of a soggy sandwich that tasted like dog shit.

The humidity was very intense, but I was eager and ready to go on a Mission. I ran into my hut, put on my flight suit and grabbed my special medical bag that I kept there. This was in addition to the medical supplies that were on the Medevac Helicopter. I ran towards the Chopper as the Crew Chief was yelling, "Hurry up, we're ready to go".

I climbed aboard. The Crew Chief told me to hang on. In a Chopper, this was a sound warning as the Pilot often had to take evasive measures to avoid fire from the enemy while in flight. Since the doors were always open on either side of the Helicopter, all passengers had to hold on or risk falling out of the Aircraft.

I am sure there were all kinds of safety equipment aboard the Helicopter. In the heat of the moment, when everybody concentrated on getting to the wounded, nobody worried about having his seat belt fastened.

*Doc Zoo, in door of Medevac, as it leaves LZ Uplift to pick up wounded men.*

Once airborne, the Pilot and Crew Chief asked, "How's the Doc doing?"

My reply to them was, "At your service, gentlemen".

The Pilot informed me that the flight would be short. We were going to pick up a mother and daughter outside of Binh Dinh. It seems that the girl became a victim of the Viet Cong/NVA.

Earlier, while playing like any normal child, she fell into a pit full of sharpened punji stakes (sharpened bamboo sticks used in a primitive but effective pit trap, often smeared with excrement to cause infection).

As we approached the pick up sight, I could clearly see green smoke and a number of soldiers securing the Landing Zone as we approached.

When the Chopper landed, the mother climbed aboard and a soldier handed me the wounded girl. She was crying hysterically. When she fell in the hole, the punji stake first impaled her left leg. Her normal reaction to put her right hand out to keep from falling resulted in the punji stake going through her hand, as well.

The young girl bled profusely, and since there was no Medic with the Recon Platoon that picked her up, the soldiers could only put a field dressing on the wound.

As soon as we were off the ground, I began to treat the girl. At the same time, I kept the Pilot aware of her progress. The child and her mother were both hysterical and their hygiene was less than desirable. They both smelled bad.

I gently took the girl's hand and pulled it off the punji stake. The child's mother started screaming because she thought I would hurt her daughter even more.

I reached down and removed the stick from the bottom of her foot next. I tossed the stick through the open door of the Helicopter. Then I cleaned the wounds and bandaged the child's hand and foot.

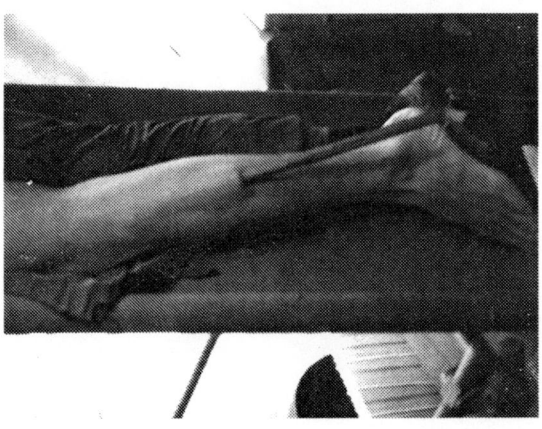

*Punji stick like this one (stuck in a Republic of Vietnam Soldier's leg) is what impaled a young Vietnamese girl's leg and hand. Doc Zoo, CO B Medical, removed the stick from the girl's hand and leg.*

Once the punji stake disappeared, the child and her mother quieted down a little. The young girl was still crying, so I offered her a piece of hard candy that my parents sent to me. She cried some more and shook her head no to my candy offer. She later finally relented and took the candy.

When she put it in her mouth and realized it was sweet tasting, she sat the rest of the trip looking out the door of the Helicopter, still sobbing, but quietly sucking on the piece of candy. She was too small for morphine, but I gave her aspirin to ease the pain from the punji stake wounds.

Here was yet another child at play who became a victim of the war. I never saw the mother or the child again and I was always curious as to how they made out. It always stuck in my mind how cruel the enemy can be.

# ROOT CANAL

After working a dozen Medcaps, I started flying on a regular basis as a Dustoff (Medevac) Medic. It was a cool job because I had a lot of time to myself. However, I had to be available at a moment's notice to respond to an emergency. On the average, the flights would take a half-hour to forty-five minutes round trip from Company B Medical to the pick-up point and back. Ninety percent of the time, the Landing Zone would be secured by the time the Medevac Helicopter arrived to pick up the wounded.

One day, on our way to a routine pick-up in the jungle, a heavy rain started to fall. The soldier waiting for the Medevac had a root canal problem. As the Chopper neared the pick up sight, the winds blew up and the sky became very dark. The Chopper shuddered as it strained against the incoming storm. I began to wonder if we were going to make it to the Medevac sight.

*Inside Dustoff Helicopter, Co B Medical.*

Suddenly, the radio came alive. It was the pilot announcing that, "We are going down, now!" I thought, "We're hit!" I did not hear any gunfire or heavy artillery, however. It was more like the Helicopter just decided to shut itself down.

The last thing I remember was one of the Pilots saying, "We're going to auto rotate, so hang on". We hit a few branches on the way down, but the landing did not seem to be that difficult.

The Crew Chief was immediately out of the Aircraft and had the engine cover off trying to find the problem. The Pilot and Co-Pilot were off the Chopper after calling in a Mayday and giving our location.

I knew there was NVA/Viet Cong in the area and I grew nervous. One of the Pilots said it was only a little bit farther to pick up the Root Canal Soldier and he hoped that someone in the sick man's Platoon saw us land and would come to our rescue.

Minutes went by. There was no hope of restarting the Chopper. The Root Canal Soldier's Platoon showed up (the guy with the toothache in tow). They told us we would have to leave the disabled Helicopter and board another Chopper. In response to our Mayday, the Chopper was on its way to our location.

I asked one of the Sergeants, "Where's the guy with the tooth problem?" I figured that in the few moments, while waiting for our ride, I would examine the ailing soldier.

The Sergeant brought the soldier to me. He looked like he just stepped out of the Movie, "Deliverance". He smelled bad and was ornery as hell.

When I asked to let me look at his tooth, the Soldier yelled, "Does this guy know what the fuck he's doing?" The swollen side of his face looked a mess and I am sure that the Soldier was in a lot of pain.

I thought it looked like someone took a thirty-two-ounce Louisville Slugger and put his face out in left field.

My mood was not exactly cheerful, after crashing in the Helicopter and I took offense to his comment. My nerves felt like a bungee cord stretched to the max. Okay, I could see that the Soldier was in a lot of pain, but I still was not going to take any shit from him. I told him to trust me and sit down so I could look at the tooth. I assured him, that when a Chopper showed up to take us back to the LZ, he would be on it. He really had a bad attitude, but he agreed.

I asked him to open his mouth. I could see his injury was more than a tooth infection. I found a hole behind his cheek that penetrated to the inside of his mouth. He also had puncture wounds on his body.

It looked like a grenade or a land mine hit him. The explosives chewed him up. I asked him how long he was in this condition. He responded, "Three days".

I asked the Soldier where his Medic was. He said he died a few days ago. That sadly made sense. The chances of a Medic surviving in the field were not good, because the NVA/Viet Cong always tried to kill them or the Radioman first.

I bandaged some of his other wounds. "We will be picked up soon". I reassured him.

A few moments later, four Helicopters were overhead. They landed and extracted everyone. One of the Helicopters stayed behind to guard the disabled Air Craft.

The Soldier whose "root canal" I treated thanked me upon our return to Company B Medical. His demeanor was much more friendly towards me now. He told me, "Dig it, Zoo, brother. We have to get together and party sometime".

It was a few weeks later. I was walking across LZ Uplift when I ran into one of the Sergeants that helped with the downed Helicopter.

I asked him how the Soldier was with the "abscessed tooth". He stopped dead in his tracks and looked me dead in the eyes and said, "He's all gone. He was killed in a fire fight the night before last". I thought to myself, "His dental problems were the least of his worries". I then said a silent prayer for him.

# Last Dustoff (Medevac) Mission

Of the forty-seven missions that I flew as a Dustoff (Medevac) Medic, the majority of wounds that I treated were from shrapnel, gun shots, and many other non life threatening wounds that, if not treated, could become life threatening. Only a half dozen or so times did I encounter a seriously injured person who was in danger of dying from their wounds. Though I liked the job as Dustoff (Medevac) Medic, it began to bring me down after a while.

Seeing so much misery on a daily basis became very difficult to bear. It seemed like I performed countless months of Dustoff (Medevac) runs and Medcaps before my assignment to the Aid Station to pull other Medcaps. The Medcaps, where I went to the local villages to treat people, constituted the basis of a great deal of the Brigade's Assistance Programs called "Civic Action".

The Brigade also had a program called "Dentcap", where a Dental Technician would go with me on my Medcaps. A lot of time, beyond treating the sick and injured people in the villages, we also gave them soap, medical supplies, candy, and food. In some areas, the specific "Civic Action" programs became more elaborate, with the building of schools, roads, bridges, and establishing Girl Scout Troops. These were often joint projects shared by the Americans and the Republic of Vietnam.

*A Republic of Vietnam Girl Scout Troop in Bong Song. They are part of Civil Action.*

I started to enjoy going out and helping villagers in different locations and providing the refugees with whatever help I could give them. One day as I was packing to go out, my Senior NCO asked me if I would fly Dustoff (Medevac) for the day, as the other Medic was sick. He said we could hold off on the Medcap until another day, especially since there was a threat of thunderstorms in the area.

It was a little after lunchtime. I just finished eating, when a Dustoff (Medevac) call came in to pick up a wounded soldier. He was near the South China Sea. From what the Pilot of the Medevac Helicopter told me, the soldier's wounds were not too severe. The trip started out as a routine Dustoff (Medevac) Mission. We were flying along the coastline and I thought to myself how beautiful the beaches looked and how nice this place might be if there was not a war.

As we made our descent into the pick up sight, the Pilot made a sharp left turn and I could see purple smoke on the ground.

I heard the Pilot say, "I identify purple smoke". Then the Pilot said, "I see two purple smokes, each in a different location. It looks like the NVA is trying to get us to land near them."

It seemed that the NVA/Viet Cong also threw out a purple smoke grenade to try to confuse our Chopper Pilot as to where to land. (A smoke grenade releases brightly colored smoke. They are good for signaling choppers that the landing zone is either secure or hot).

*Dustoff pick-up near South China Sea.*

Someone launched a red smoke grenade right on top of the purple grenade. I heard the Pilot say, "I identify purple and red smoke".

The ground unit radioed back, "Roger that, come on in". When I heard the Helicopter Pilot call for Gun ship support, I knew this was going to turn into a hot Landing Zone. Everything happened so fast, that we were on the ground before I even knew it.

We could hear gunfire in the distance. It was our own Troops trying to keep the enemy at bay as we loaded the wounded soldier into the Helicopter.

The Pilot had the Medevac Helicopter at full throttle on the ground. There was gunfire all around us. We were in the doorway of the Helicopter urging the two soldiers who were helping the wounded man to hurry up. We could hear the bullets pinging off the shell of the aircraft.

We got the Patient on the Helicopter in lightning speed and wasted no time in taking off. At that point, my heart was in my throat. We were only about ten feet off the ground. I was holding onto the wounded soldier when a big thump came from the rear of the aircraft. Gunfire hit somewhere in the back, which damaged a hydraulic line. Smoke started bellowing into the aircraft. All I heard the Pilot say was, "We're hit and we're going down, hold on"

I do believe that the Pilot was trying to auto rotate the aircraft to slow us down before we crashed. In a matter of seconds, however, we hit hard on the ground.

I was still attached to the communications cord and hanging by my neck off the side of the Helicopter. I was between shocked and scared to death. All I knew is I had to get loose from the cord that was choking me and cutting off my air. I reached back to pull on the cord to release the tension from my neck. It snapped and freed me. I fell from the aircraft and landed on the skids.

The NVA/Viet Cong started shooting at me from the edge of the jungle that bordered the LZ that we had established in a rice paddy. I drew my 38-caliber pistol and returned two shots before realizing that I was fucked! It was like going up against Godzilla with a BB gun.

In panic, I retreated to the rear of the aircraft to get around to the other side for more protection. In my haste, I forgot about the rear rotor blade that was still spinning. I ran right into it. Fortunately, it only caught the side of my helmet. It did shear off part of the face guard and shaved the paint down to the fiberglass, however. I was lucky that the helmet was still on my head. This was not my idea of a pleasant afternoon.

After almost shitting my pants again, I got to the other side of the Helicopter. I thought to myself, "Boy, are we fucked now".

At that point, the Pilot was out of his seat, trying to release the Co-Pilot's harness. Hit by hostile fire, there was blood everywhere from the Co-Pilot's bullet wounds. The Crew Chief and I climbed aboard the Helicopter to try to assist in freeing the wounded Co-Pilot.

Then, two Gun ships came to our rescue. The Pilot of one the Gun ships waved to me to hurry up and come on as he touched down on the ground.

Meanwhile the other Gun ship was firing its Mini guns to cover us. I left the cockpit of the downed Helicopter and helped the wounded soldier (which we had originally picked up) to the waiting Rescue Gun ship. The gunshot wound in his hand bled through the bandages wrapped around it. I had the Crew Chief of the Gun ship hold the soldiers hand up to elevate while I returned to the downed Helicopter. I was not leaving anyone behind.

The downed Helicopter and the Gun ship were about twenty-five feet apart. As I returned to the damaged aircraft, all hell broke loose.

Someone called in the big guns to fire on the enemy position while we continued the rescue. Artillery fire shook the earth all around us while we worked to extricate the body of the dead Aircraft Commander from the downed Helicopter.

We had to get our asses out of there, fast! The three of us, the Pilot, Crew Chief and I, carried the dead Co-Pilot to the waiting Gun Ship. Once aboard, we were airborne immediately.

Although, the whole ordeal maybe lasted fifteen or twenty minutes, it seemed like it was hours of pure hell.

Everyone was silent on the way back to Company B Medical. I removed the helmet from the dead Co-Pilot's head and started to cry.

As I glanced around the aircraft, it seemed that everybody was staring at me in agreement that the whole situation sucks. To that point, in Vietnam, that was as close to death as I ever wanted to be.

After we returned to Company B Medical, I walked back to my quarters, took off my flight suit, and sat on the edge of my bunk.

Though I did not know him, I was very devastated by the Co-Pilot's death. My whole brain shut down. I could not put two thoughts together. Grief paralyzed me. I thought to myself that I never wanted to fly another Dustoff (Medevac) Mission.

I waited until the next day, and talked it over with my Senior NCO. He agreed that I had my fair share of flying and that I needed a break from it. He told me to just continue my job at the Aid Station. He also wanted me to start showing the new Medics that were arriving soon, the ropes about how Company B Medical operated.

During this stage of my tour I was feeling very taxed and stressed out. Adding to the misery was the fact that I was hornier than a bull with no opportunity for sexual release. Little did I know that the real fun was just about to begin when I met "The Boys".

# Meet The Boys

After months and months and months of working in the Aid Station, pulling Medcaps and flying Dustoff (Medevac) Missions, my nerves became a little frail from the amount of people I saw wounded, the blood, the horror. Sometimes good came out of it, but not too often and I was always prepared for the worst.

Finally one day while working in the Aid Station, I saw a field Medic come in on a Dustoff (Medevac), all banged up and I just looked in his eyes and I knew what kind of life he lived.

I thought to myself, "This I must do. I must be a part of this. I have the medical skills and I have the knowledge. I do not know if I have the guts to take care of an Airborne Rifle Platoon. Being in the jungles under hostile conditions and standing up to a highly trained enemy force is a challenge".

One day while working in the Aid Station, Staff Sergeant Ray appeared. He was in charge of all the Medics as Senior NCO for Company B Medical. He treated all the Medics like gold. When the Combat Medics came back from the field he would cook up a storm for them.

It remained a mystery about how he managed to get the food to LZ Uplift. The menu often included chicken, steak or hamburgers and hot dogs.

I asked Staff Sergeant Ray for a moment of his time. I wanted to know if there was an opening in the field and if he would consider putting me out there. He looked at me and said, "You're serious, aren't you?"

I said, "Most definitely".

He said, " I know you're crazy now. You are definitely trying to get yourself killed. Why would you ever want to leave the good job that you have right now? I need you back here in the Aid Station. You are an excellent Medic. You do everything I need you to do and I just put you in for Sergeant. The field is no place for you, or for anyone else, for that matter. It will eat you alive. However, if that is what you want, okay. I'll see what I can do for you".

He walked away; shaking his head and wearing a disgusted look on his face. I heard him say, "The sorry mother fucker definitely stepped on his dick this time".

*Staff Sergeant Ray feeds hungry combat Medics when they return from the field.*

A few days later, I was at the Aid Station. I finished up on a soldier's leg that was infected. We had to wait for the paperwork to send him back to his Command.

Staff Sergeant Ray came into the Aid Station. He said, "When you get a chance, I want to talk to you, Zoo". After I sent the wounded soldier on his way, I asked Staff Sergeant Ray, "What could I do for you, Sergeant?"

He said, "Start packing a rucksack and get ready to go out to the field. I have two openings. I do not know where you are going yet. However, whoever gets you will be one lucky dog. I have to send one of the new Medics out with you. Can you keep an eye on him until he is established? I hate putting him out to the Lions this quick, but I have no choice".

I spent the next couple days packing everything that I could think of, including a well rounded fire fight bag with enough bandages, sutures, tourniquets, morphine, IV's, and just about everything imaginable to do battle field surgery on at least fifteen to twenty people if need be.

After putting everything in its proper perspective, I made sure I had enough canteens of water, food, and some personal items. I especially made sure I was well armed. I wanted to be ready to turn the enemy's dreams into nightmares.

I then wrote a letter to my parents to tell them that I was going out in the field and would not be working at the Aid Station any longer. I asked them not to worry because I would be with some tough soldiers who would watch over me.

After that, I took a short walk around the perimeter lines of LZ Uplift. I stopped at one of the perimeter bunkers to talk to one of the soldiers that I recognized as a patient at the Aid Station. He was friendly and invited me up to chat. It seemed like a nice quiet evening, so I took him up on his offer. He asked, "No Aid Station tonight, Doc?"

I said, "No, I'm going out in the field in a day or so. I'm just packing my shit to be ready to go when they tell me".

He said, "Well, good luck to you, wherever you go. By the way, did you know that the life expectancy of a Medic under fire is around seven seconds?"

I looked at him and said, "What? Where did you get your statistics from?"

He said, "Oh, yeah, it's well known that Combat Medics don't last too long in the jungle".

*This really got my attention. I left and began a search for weapons. I grabbed anything I could get my hands on. I thought to myself, "These fuckers want to kill me. I will give them a war they won't fucking believe".*

As the evening progressed, I managed to obtain a couple pistols. After I helped the Supply Sergeant out with an infected tooth, he was more than glad to supply me with the weaponry I felt I needed.

I retired to my quarters. I felt comfortable because I supplied myself well with arms. I was ready for anything that faced me in the future. What I did not have, I figured I would get when I arrived in the jungle.

As I was falling asleep, I had a smirk on my face, and I thought, "I can't wait". I was like a kid with a new toy.

I wondered how the new Platoon would greet me and what they were like. I prayed to God, "Please let me stand tall for these gentlemen". I did not know what to expect.

A new dawn began. Staff Sergeant Ray approached me and asked if that was my rucksack sitting on the side of the building. He laughed to himself and said, "Shit, man, you aren't going to be able to carry that. That stuff must weigh one hundred fifty pounds".

I looked at him and said, "Aw, I'm not worried. I can carry that". I picked the rucksack up and put it on. I thought to myself that it weighed more than I expected. I walked about fifteen yards with it on my back. "It was fucking heavy!" I lightened it up as much as I could without sacrificing the necessities and was ready to go.

It was early afternoon. The soldier from the radio room came over to me outside the Aid Station and told me to get ready, that my Helicopter ride would be arriving in a few minutes.

I waited with excitement. Staff Sergeant Ray came over to me and said, "Keep your head down and your powder dry". I saw the Helicopter approach the landing pad near the Aid Station. Imaginary thoughts channeled through my head as to what might take place in my new surroundings. I boarded a 1st Air Calvary Gun ship Helicopter that was my taxi to the jungle.

A serious thrill of excitement rushed through my body. The flight lasted fifteen minutes and I could hardly wait until we landed.

The Crew Chief yelled, "Hang on, we'll be setting down shortly, Doc".

I looked out the open section of the Aircraft and could see red smoke in the distance. (Red is a hot LZ). This showed where the Landing Zone was. I hoped that it was secure. As I deployed from the Aircraft, a half dozen of my new Platoon met me and quickly whisked me into the jungle. Most of our operations occurred in areas already sprayed with Agent Orange and Agent White.

We caught up to the rest of the under manned Platoon in the jungle. My welcome was not enthusiastic. The first two soldiers I met were Don and "The Big Hawaiian".

I overheard a couple soldiers say, "I hope the fuck this clown Medic knows what he's doing".

The Lieutenant introduced himself to me and I reciprocated. Then he hustled the Platoon to get on the move. I did not have a chance to really talk to any of the Platoon before we began our hump.

As we left, I knew my damn rucksack would catch up to me sooner, not later. We had to cross an eight hundred meter long rice paddy dike. About one third across, my legs started giving out. The rucksack now felt like it weighed a ton. Everybody bitched at me to stay with the Platoon, as I asked if we could take a break. Several of the men voiced amazement at my naiveté and said in unison. "We can't take a break here, we're in the middle of a rice paddy!"

I gathered every drop of strength both mentally and physically. Finally, our Platoon reached the jungle's edge. I sat down and took a drink of water. One of my Platoon members told me, "Don't worry, you'll get used to it.

I said to myself, "How the fuck do you ever get used to this?" I looked around at the bunch of very battle worn soldiers. They had a very aggressive manner. It was almost like something in a movie, only you are in it.

I did not make friends quickly, at first. Throughout the course of the day, however, one man then another came and asked for a band-aid or an aspirin. I could see they were trying to figure out what kind of Medic I was going to be and what I was like. I did not know their previous Medic. From all I heard, however, he was damn good. I hoped that I could live up to his standards.

The Lieutenant said, "Well, Doc, did you have enough rest because we have to get going?"

Little did I know that I was in for the worst day of my life. I slipped my arms under the rucksack. Soon I became aware that I did not have enough strength to pick the fucking thing up. Now, I had to go to Plan B. I had to roll over on my stomach, and have two soldiers help me up to my feet. Once I was up, I could feel the rucksack digging into my neck like a dull knife. I said, "Holy shit, man. Somebody help me with this fucking rucksack. It's cutting my neck".

One of my Platoon members took pity on me. He said, "Let's shift Doc's rucksack around, and get a towel to put under the bar so it doesn't dig into his neck".

Someone else mumbled, "Cherry fucker".

I said, "I'm not a Cherry. I've been in country for over a year". Another guy said, "You been in country over a year, where the hell ya been then?" I explained I worked in the Company B Medical Aid Station and flew Dustoff (Medevac). They fixed my rucksack. I asked, "How much farther do we have to fucking go before we rest for the evening?"

A mean, nasty looking soldier, spit a wad of chew on the ground and wiped the juice off his face with a long knife. He looked like a fucking Pirate.

He said, "See the top of that mountain, boy? That's where we'll be tonight". Although we had to take a break about every hundred yards for my rucksack, my Platoon members decided not to kill me. It surprised me because they had three good reasons; namely their total aggravation with the jungle, knowing we were surrounded by the NVA/Viet Cong, and having a Medic who could not carry his rucksack.

Half way through the day, we met up with another Platoon from the same Company. Someone from that Platoon recognized me from the Aid Station. He said, "Isn't that the guy from Company B Medical?"

I looked at him and replied, "Yeah".

He asked, "What are you doing out here? You had it made at the Aid Station".

I answered, "I want to see what the world out here is really like".

He replied, "Welcome to hell!"

We met up with another Platoon. I knew a few of them from the Aid Station, also and they were telling my new Platoon members what a good Medic I was.

We took a break, while the Platoon Leaders looked over maps. I administered health care to both Platoons while we were resting.

I asked some of my Platoon members, "Where the hell is your Medic?"

The reply came that the two previous Medics from both Platoons finished their tour of duty and went home. I was the only one qualified to be in the field so I administered health care to both the $2^{nd}$ and $3^{rd}$ Platoons.

We stayed at that location for another forty-five minutes before the Platoon Leaders signaled us to pack up because we were moving to a different location.

I finally got back on my feet with the help of my new Platoon members. I was sure the rucksack somehow doubled in weight since I left the Aid Station.

We were in a flat area, in the 506 Valley. After more breaks and more bitching from other Platoon members about me, one soldier asked, "Is there a problem that he can't keep up?"

"Yea, man, did you see the size of his fucking rucksack?"

I replied in frustration, "Yea, man, it's all your Medical shit to keep you fuckers alive". I started getting a severe "case of the ass" and they knew I was not going to take any more shit from anybody. Out of nowhere came a quiet remark, "I wonder if the fucker can fight. He's got enough weapons".

That really pissed me off! It almost started a gunfight between all of us. Our Platoon Leader broke in by saying, "What the fuck you people think you're doing? We got five thousand fucking NVA out here trying to kill us and you fuckers are trying to kill each other for no reason. Leave the Doc alone. Just remember, you might need him quick and remember your first fucking day in this hellhole. You guys weren't the cream of the crop when you first arrived, either".

Things chilled out and we all laughed. "It's just the fucking heat man. This place sucks!"

Later in the afternoon, the heat index was at full max. Though we felt like we were in the tropic of hell, everything was cool between all of us soldiers.

Every bone in my body hurt. I was to the point of tears, from the pain of carrying my rucksack and wondering when the hell we would ever get to our destination. After more breaks and more bitching, we finally reached our objective. It was an old burned out village.

I thought to myself, "You mean we came all the way here for nothing?" There were no Viet Cong in site, nor was there a breath of fresh air. We all took a break in what little shade we could find while the Platoon Leaders decided what to do next.

Through the course of this break, some of the other soldiers from the Platoon introduced themselves to me and asked me questions as they tried to get a feel for who I was.

Later, I opened a can of beans and franks and broke off a piece of C-4 from a Claymore mine. I lit a match and set the C-4 on fire, then held the can by the lid over the flame.

(C-4 is great for heating your food, as long you do not blow yourself up. C-4 is a plastic, putty textured explosive carried by infantry soldiers. You can light it. It can boil water in seconds. Just don't stomp on it as it takes compression to explode. Other uses are to heat rations in the field and for blowing up bunkers).

It was getting later in the day. Our Platoon Leader decided we would set up camp where we were. We could see a Piper Cub gathering aerial photographs of enemy movements to radio their positions back to Command Headquarters.

The best news I heard all day was that we would camp here for the evening. I could have cried for joy because at that point, I was just about to curse the day my mother gave me birth because of that heavy rucksack.

As I laid back and tried to rest, different soldiers came to me and complained about injuries, illnesses, and whatever was hurting them. I really did not get much chance to sleep. By then, the soreness in my body from the march and carrying the rucksack really set in. I thought to my self, "If tomorrow is the same as today, I'll be dead by the end of the week".

The next day, I was so sore I could barely move. I managed to give sick call. I looked at my rucksack and applied every way I could think of to pad the straps and the shoulder bar. A couple of the Boys gave me suggestions on how to add padding to make life a little bit easier on the constitution. After sick call every body grabbed a quick breakfast and the Lieutenant said, "Okay, men, let's get ready to move out".

Once again, the rucksack weighed so much that I could not pick it up let alone stand up with it on my back. Some of the Platoon Members helped me to my feet and the rotten day began again.

We walked for an hour before the soreness started loosening up, but I was dead ass tired. Lucky the Platoon Leader told us, "Hold up, and everybody take a break. But keep a close eye on your surroundings". We could sense there was danger close by, in the jungle. Everyone was on full alert.

We rested for a few minutes and drank some water from our canteens. Some soldiers grabbed a quick bite to eat. The Lieutenant said, "We're going to move out in a few minutes because we will be extracted to a new location.

Command thought that the enemy was in this area. However, they either moved to another location or were possibly underground in their well-built tunnels. The NVA based their defensive strategy mainly on ways of escaping.

They would split up in well-organized groups, going in different directions. In some cases, they used extremely well built underground tunnels that took years and years to construct and went for miles and miles. The whole NVA Army was pretty much underground, as they had hospitals, their communications and food supplies in these tunnels. Built well, with steel and concrete, our artillery or jet fire could not penetrate them. The NVA even had tunnels under Phu Cat Air Force Base.

When Bob Hope came to Nam to visit the Troops, the NVA had tunnels underneath the stage where he performed. The Americans had their Christmas Party at the base and later found evidence that the NVA were having a party in the tunnel beneath them.

The NVA also had caches of weapons outside their tunnels. They could organize a raid efficiently. The NVA soldier would crawl out of the tunnel, collect his weapons from the cache and be ready for battle. The NVA Squad leaders blew whistles to organize their Platoons. It was a scary sound for a Platoon of Americans to hear those whistles blowing and echoing through the jungle.

Mostly, the NVA used the whistles in a Company size or large attack against the Americans. The enemy hoped they could intimidate the 173$^{rd}$ Airborne Troops by blowing whistles.

I sat and looked at my rucksack and thought to myself, "This dirty fucker is not going to get the best of me today". Then a wonderful idea came into my head. I spotted a little tree that was right by my rucksack. I sat down, put my arms in the straps, rolled over to my knees, grabbed a hold of the tree, and pulled myself up. What a moment of triumph! I got up on my own with the rucksack.

We started down a small path towards a clearing where an extraction could take place. All of a sudden, we ran smack into a half dozen or so NVA Soldiers coming up the same path from the opposite direction. They literally ran right into us. We wasted no time in destroying all of them. One of our men caught bullets in his shoulder and leg. Before Medic came out of his mouth, I was there tending to his wounds.

The Lieutenant yelled, "Doc, how is he".

I yelled back, "He's okay, he'll make it".

Now instead of an extraction to a different location, we needed a Dustoff (Medevac) Helicopter. As I continued tending the soldier's wounds, I used forceps to remove a piece of shrapnel from his leg the size of a quarter. Since it did not hit an artery, the blood clotted on its own with direct pressure. The soldier was not complaining, but asked me "How bad am I hit, Doc?"

I said, "Enough to get you Dustoff (Medevac) and get you out of here, but you will be okay".

I gave him a shot of morphine to ease the pain and turned my attention to a less serious wound in his shoulder. I started an IV and treated him for shock. "I assured him that everything was fine and that I was there for him". The Lieutenant asked for a body count of the enemy we just killed. Then he ordered the Platoon to secure the area and Doc while he worked on the wounded Soldier.

After I did as much as possible for the soldier, he put out his hand and thanked me. I said, "No problem, man, that's my job".

A Medevac Helicopter landed at the Extraction Sight that we secured. We got the wounded man aboard. Once aboard the Helicopter, I remembered that I forgot to make out a tag of what time I gave the Soldier the Morphine. I yelled to the Dustoff (Medevac) Medic, the time, and the dosage. The Medic shook his ahead in acknowledgement and wrote out the tag.

We all took a short break while waiting for a Helicopter ride to a different location. My biggest fear of how I would react in the first firefight no longer was an issue. The rest of the Platoon seemed pleased with my performance and thanked me for doing a good job.

That was the turning point in our friendship. After that event, we became closer as a Platoon and shared a comradeship that we did not have before.

As the days went on, we traveled through the jungle looking for the enemy. Command got reports of enemy movements given to us by aerial reconnaissance and local informants.

In addition, CID (Central Investigation Detachment) members would go out in small Platoons to gather as much information about the enemy as possible. They often worked in conjunction with S.O.G. (Studies and Observation Group).

The Monsoon season was upon us. It starts at the end of September and goes to early December. Every day at about noon, it would start raining and continue on the rest of the day into the evening. This went on day and night for months. Amid all the other shit we had to deal with, the Monsoon makes everything fucking worse. Whatever you are wearing is soaked all the time. Rashes and other skin ailments, malaria, and just being cold and wet made life practically unbearable.

My suggestion to everyone was to keep your feet as dry as possible and use medicated foot powder. One day after taking a break, a FNG (Fuckin' New Guys) came up to me and said, "Hey, Doc, can you look at my head".

I put down the poncho liner that I was folding and said, "Let me take a look".

At first, I could not see anything wrong with his head and I asked him, "What seems to be the problem?"

He pulled a patch of hair out of his head and then another, then another. We took him back to LZ Uplift. The Doctors were amazed at what they saw. No one knew how to cure him and eventually he went completely bald. They sent the soldier to Qui Nhon Hospital for further evaluation.

Whatever they did for him, his hair grew back within six months. I think the poor guy needed a break from the war. His hair loss was probably due to a case of bad nerves.

# THE KING COBRA

## March 1969

---

It was the middle of the month. I was about to embark on one of my early missions into the field as a combat Medic. My Orders were to go out with the personnel of the 3rd Platoon on a mission for a few days. Their Medic was ill and so they were borrowing me.

The 1st AV BDE Helicopters were on their way to pick us up. They performed all of our airlifts. We waited for them at the extraction sight. They were going to transport us to an undisclosed location on a search and destroy mission.

The Helicopters landed on time, we boarded them quickly, and off we went to our destination. The whole time we were flying, about twenty-five minutes, I wondered to myself where we were going and for how long.

I did not know anyone in the 3rd Platoon. They were glad to have an experienced Medic in their Platoon, however. A small Friendly force (American Troops) waited for our arrival.

I could see the green from the smoke grenades and hear the pilot confirm the color. He got ready for his final descent into the rice paddy. I heard him say, "Get ready, men. I am only touching down for a second. So get off my damn Helicopter as fast as you can".

I jumped off the Helicopter, as did the rest of the Platoon. We were on the ground in seconds. Adrenaline flooded my body so fast that it became outrageous. I knew we were in for a long, adventurous day.

We met up with other members of the Aco 1/503$^{rd}$ Inf at the base of the jungle. From there, we broke up into three Platoons of eight to ten men each. We then headed in different directions. My Squad walked along a rice paddy dike, which makes you very vulnerable to the enemy.

Before we could get into the cover of the jungle, a huge King Cobra appeared from nowhere. At first, everyone was so petrified of the eight foot snake, that the men tried to get out of its way, as it raced around the members of my Platoon in front of me.

Within a blink of the eye, the snake slithered its way to my position. It raised itself up to full height and flared out its hood. I found myself standing face to face staring into its eyes and horrified, as well. The beauty of the snake mesmerized me. It was black, silver with a little red, and yellow. It seemed like its eyes were as big as mine. I knew that if I attempted to make even a small movement, or even breathe, I was instantly dead.

The snake looked me over by slowly moving its head back and forth in front of my face, as if deciding whether to strike or not. At that point, I believe I became scared beyond shitless. The snake stood there, (I say stood, because it seemed that the snake was standing on his tail) for about three more seconds in front of my face. Then it dropped down and like a phantom, it vanished into the jungle.

The soldiers behind me were petrified. No one ever saw a standoff between a soldier and a Cobra before. Immediately, the four men behind me opened fire on the retreating snake. Bullets flew everywhere and ricocheted off the ground. I felt like I was in a shooting gallery. No body hit the snake, but they almost killed each other and me.

*A King Cobra like this one tried to hypnotize Doc Zoo.*

I could hear one of the Platoon Leaders screaming. "Stop shooting! They know we are here now. Let's get the hell out of here". We did.

After we regained our composure from the Kamikaze snake terror, we continued our mission.

# The Straightjacket

## June 1970

---

The Battalion Commander required everyone to take pills to prevent malaria. It was the Medic's responsibility to enforce that rule. The Malaria rate began to skyrocket. Many people became sick due to extended stays in the jungle. I usually handed out the weekly large red malaria pill on Monday and then a little white pill each day thereafter. I also made sure the men swallowed the pills.

Even taking the pill did not guarantee you would not get malaria. I found this out first hand. One morning, as the sun just barley rose to the horizon, I began giving sick call. I did not feel too well. Half way through sick call, I started burning up with fever. It made me feel like I was on the outskirts of hell.

Gary said to me, "Hey Zoo, you don't look too good". I went to my aid bag, pulled out a thermometer, and stuck it in my mouth. My Platoon members were asking if I was okay. The Lieutenant confronted me as I removed the thermometer. It read 104 degrees.

The next thing I remember, a couple of soldiers helped me onto a Dustoff (Medevac) and put my rucksack and rifle on with me. They kept my medical equipment with them. They had a Helicopter fly me back to LZ Uplift for an evaluation. I arrived delirious and just heard little bits and pieces of what the doctor said. A Medevac Helicopter and another Medic flew me to Qui Nhon Hospital, which was forty-five miles south of Bong Song.

The next thing I know, some one told me to put my arms out straight. When I did that, they slipped a straightjacket on me. I did not like that at all. At this point, several Medics tried to put me in a tub of ice water to bring my fever down. Once my ass hit the ice water I went into a direct, positive pissed off mode.

I was determined to get out of the straightjacket at all costs. At one point, I was trying to dislocate my shoulder, like Houdini, and set myself free. The harder they tried to hold me the more I struggled. The last thing I remember was one of the Medics yelling, "Mother of God, he's getting loose".

In my delirium, I must have threatened to kill all those people who were trying to help me. When I woke up, I had a bunch of people standing around me. I asked them, "Why am I in this straightjacket?" I looked down and saw an IV attached to my leg instead of my arm.

One of the Medics said, "Are you okay?"

I asked again, "What seems to be the problem?"

He answered, "Well, you were going to kill everyone last night. It seems you are back on earth this morning. I think we can remove the straightjacket".

As they removed the straightjacket, the Medic told me I had the less serious type of Malaria but that it could reoccur. They also told me that the other type of malaria, if you live through it, you would never get it again.

I thought to myself, "I sure as hell hope that I never have to suffer from a bout of Malaria again. I think that no one should have to endure an experience with that disease. Who would ever want to be thrown into a state of sweat, hallucinations, and temporary insanity?"

Later, I returned to my Platoon in the jungle. It seems funny that the only one in my Squad that got Malaria was the Medic.

# The Boa

We came in on stand down one day (an infantry unit's return from the jungle to the base camp for refitting and training).

Many people were eligible for R & R (Rest and Relaxation) for which they were long over due. Because we were down to the basics of what a Platoon or a Company should be in manpower, we had many FNGs just coming "in country",

Many wounded men went back to the States. Other soldier's tours of duty were over. I requested an R & R to Hawaii, which I heard was one of the better places to go. I was packing to go there when Doug and Danny approached me. They were in D Company 1st/503rd Airborne Infantry. I knew them from previous battles we fought together against the enemy in the jungle.

Doug said, "Hey, Zoo, how would you like to be a great guy and switch R & R's with me?" I looked at him like, "What are you nuts?"

He replied, "Zoo, my wife just had a baby boy. If I can go to Hawaii, her father will give them the money to fly over from Oregon for the week".

"Where is your R & R, Doug?" I asked. "Thailand", he rejoined.

I thought about for a moment, and knowing Doug to be a good person, I said, "Okay".

Doug was overwhelmed with joy when I agreed to trade tickets. He now had to get to where he could place a MARS (Military Affiliated Radio System) call to tell his wife the good news. Forward Command Post at LZ English is where you made a call. He had to get a Helicopter ride there to telephone.

Danny said, "Zoo, this is great. Me and you are going to Thailand together and we're going to have a fucking blast!"

We each had close to one thousand dollars, which is more than enough money to have the time of our lives. For me, all I wanted to do is just get away from the war and forget I ever heard about Nam for a couple of days. It seemed like my mind was disassembling.

I needed some peace and quiet. I needed to get my mind out of the jungles, off firefights, wounded soldiers, and looking for Viet Cong.

As I packed and got ready to leave, Staff Sergeant Ray, from Company B Medical, said to me, "Hey Zoo, enjoy your self in Hawaii".

I replied, "Sarge, you're not going to believe this but I traded my R & R with some one else, so he could go visit his family".

With his usual saying, "The sorry mother fucker is gonna get himself in some trouble now! I just know it".

I looked at him and said, "You worry about me too much".

Sergeant Ray was in charge of all the combat medics and really loved every one of us. He said, "Just be careful".

I boarded a Huey Gun ship that was giving Danny and I a ride down to Qui Nhon Air Base. From there, we waited for ten minutes and then caught a Cargo flight further south to a bigger military installation at Cam Rahn Bay.

From there, we waited about half an hour and we boarded a flight to Bangkok, Thailand. It was a short flight. The scenery was the same as in Vietnam, but we were still thrilled to leave that country and get on some friendly territory.

When we got through customs, we exchanged our MPC's (Military Pay Vouchers) for the local currency (bot). The largest bill was worth five dollars in Thai money. Once we got our money situated, we were free to go our own way.

As we walked out of the airport, a man who looked liked Ho Chi Minh yelled "Taxi, Taxi". He was driving an old beat up Fiat. His teeth were black from chewing beetle nut (a mild sedative).

He asked, "Where you go, GI? I take you. I take you both where you want to go". We got in the Taxi and directed the driver to the best Hotel in Bangkok. Though it was clean, it was not the Plaza in New York City. Moreover, there was no air conditioning.

The Taxi driver wanted to wait around to take us wherever we wanted to go for the time we would be there.

We told him, "No, we want to go out on our own".

The Taxi driver left. We had a few beers at the hotel bar while we waited for the clerk to check us in and have our luggage delivered to our room.

My first thought was, "Let's get up to the fucking room with our luggage before they rob us blind".

By the time we got to our room, the bellhop was standing there with a shit-eating grin on his face saying, "First time in Bangkok?" I looked at him and thought to myself, "Get the fuck out of this room before it's your last time in Bangkok". I just wanted to take a shower and have a few minutes alone.

The shit-eating grin came back to the bellhop's face and he said, "GI want beer? I go get beer".

Danny gave him so money and told him to bring back as much cold beer as the money would buy. He no sooner left than another knock came on the door. It was a different bellhop. He asked, "GI want Marijuana?"

Danny said, "Come on, get in here you little fucker and close the door".

I said, "Yes, we would like some".

His reply was, "What kind of Marijuana would you like?"

I looked at Danny, then at the bellhop. I smiled and said, "What kind do you have?"

"Oh", the bellhop said, "I have all kinds of Marijuana for GI". He went on with a list that was as long as a restaurant menu.

I thought to myself, "Holy shit. I didn't even know there was that many kinds of Marijuana".

Danny asked him, "How much is it a bag?"

The bellhop said, "For you GI, two dollar each". Each bag weighed about one and one-half ounces. At this point, the other bellhop arrived with the cold beer. As I tipped him, I heard Danny say to the purveyor of the Grass, "Fuck it, give us a bag of each".

As the night progressed, it seemed like the paranoia of war temporarily eased. My nerves were starting to level out. After another phone call to the front desk for a much larger beer delivery this time, we decided to hit the sights of downtown Bangkok.

Bangkok seemed like a small New York City. Motorcycles, bikes, and small motorcycles that people made into buses ruled the road. I did not see any cars. Dan and I were half in the bag and wound up in a local pool hall not far from the Hotel. We were drinking Rice Wine with the locals and shooting pool with them.

We finally made it back to our room and got good nights sleep. By 8:00 A.M., we were ready to go for another day's activities.

Before we could leave our hotel room, a stream of purveyors from prostitutes, vendors selling clothes, shoe shines, massages, pedicures, and even the Marijuana Dealer returned. We told him to hit the road. We had enough pot to last us a year. We did ask one young boy to stay, as he agreed to show us around town, for a price, of course.

We went to various tourist sights and saw some beautiful Buddha Temples. We toured a Buddhist Monk's House. There, we had to remove our shoes and were admonished not to touch anything. Among the treasures, were a large, solid gold Buddha and two smaller Buddha statues. Told not to take pictures, we did anyway while no one was looking.

The sights were breath taking. I was glad that I came with someone that I knew. It seemed that we were going to have a good time for the rest of our stay. Part of the afternoon, we went shopping for gifts. I picked out things for my Mother and Father to send home and a few little items for myself.

After shopping, we returned to the Hotel to relax and freshen up. Then we went out on a wild, drunken' binge and wound up back at the pool hall by the Hotel.

I started hustling the locals for their money. They did not seem to mind at first, until I started putting a dent in their wallets. Their faces went from smiles to frowns when I continued to take their money after winning each round of pool. Danny said, "Hey Zoo, these fuckers don't look too happy". We continued to drink their Rice Wine through a straw.

I could sense the situation getting tenser as we went along. So, to make it all fair in love and war, I let them win some of their money back, just to keep the peace.

By now, everything was friendly again. Frowns went back to smiles and we started playing partners for no money.

The patrons retrieved more Rice Wine and we partied into the night. They could speak English fairly well, and seemed to like GIs. Nevertheless, my experience in the jungles of Vietnam left me paranoid enough that I still felt that I had to keep my guard up and my back to the wall.

We returned to the Hotel and got a good night's sleep. The next morning we were ready for day number three of our R & R. We ate breakfast and waited for our guide to come. I thought to myself,

"Why couldn't they send us to fuckin' Thailand instead of Vietnam for a war?"

Later, we went outside to wait for our guide. "Boy this is going to be a beautiful day". I said to Danny. He had a handful of maps and tourist guide pamphlets. He shuffled through them to see where we wanted to go first. Finally, our guide showed up. There seemed to be confusion between where he wanted to take us and where we wanted to go.

Danny wanted to go to a Zoo and I wanted to go to a museum. The guide smiled and said, "I know a place where there's both a zoo and a museum. He added, "I think there will be karate in the afternoon".

We both agreed that after we stop for a couple cold beers, the zoo and the museum would be our second stop. We arrived at the place the guide decided we would enjoy. The building that we faced had a huge, gold Buddha sitting in the front of it. Red velvet trimmed everything around it. I would remember this sight for its beauty an dignity for a long time.

Prohibited from taking pictures, and unable to sneak a photo, I had to hold that Buddha in my memory. We strolled down halls exhibiting battle armor and historic cultural items. In one room, we had to take our shoes off to enter. This room belonged to an Emperor. The room was large, with red, black and gold, and Asian furniture.

After about an hour of touring, we wound up outside in a large open area. There were refreshments and food. Danny said to me, "Hey Zoo look, there's a boxing ring over there".

It looked like this is where they had all their local Muai Tai Kick Boxing events. As we sipped on our beers, I saw people starting to gather in the bleachers surrounding the ring. I said to Danny, "Boy, this is cool. Maybe they are going to have a karate exhibition. Let's go over, get a seat, and see what happens".

Lucky to get seats close to the ring, and no admission to pay, we just sat and drank our beers until the competition began. Little did I know I would later be part of the entertainment.

The server came by and asked us if we wanted more beer. I said, "Yes, bring a couple more".

They were going down very well at that point. We saw some men bring out huge stacks of tiles and bricks. I said to Danny, "I think they're going to have a breaking demonstration".

Again, the server came by and we ordered a couple more beers. We were anticipating the show getting underway. Three Thai Martial Artists entered the ring. Two of them were holding up one inch thick by 12-inch square tiles.

Spectators packed the bleachers. They cheered the person that was going to break the tiles. As the Thai Martial Artist focused with deep breathing and concentration on the two suspended tiles, he let out a yell and leaped into the air with the grace of a cougar leaping on its prey. With a jump, spinning, back kick he instantly shattered the tiles into tiny pieces.

The crowd went nuts with applause and cheers as he was setting up for his next breaking demonstration. This time it was bricks.

The audience still applauded. My friend Danny with one, too many beers in him yelled out to the people in the ring, "He ain't shit! Put my buddy, Zoo in there. He'll show you how it's done". He kept pointing to me as they looked at him. The show continued, and the Thai broke ten bricks with a closed fist. The bricks instantly shattered into red dust.

Almost immediately, Danny opens his mouth again and yells, "Aw, Zoo can do that. That ain't that great". I said to him, "Would you please shut your mouth! You're going to get us both in a lot of trouble".

With that Danny yelled, "More beer", to the passing server. It was apparent that Danny was drunk. I did not appreciate the scene he caused. I did not want anyone's attention on me. I just wanted to relax and watch the exhibition.

Danny's yelling definitely got the attention of the Thai Martial Artists, however. They invited me to come up into the ring. At first, I refused. One of the

Thais came out of the ring and asked me if I was a black belt. When I replied, "Yes", the Thai smiled and asked, "Do you break tile?" Again, I answered in the affirmative.

I finally agreed to come into the ring and demonstrate breaking. They set up ten 12-inch square tiles on top of two cinder blocks. I was a little bit wheezy from the beer, but not drunk.

I got my focus together and broke the tiles with a force that left the audience applauding and yelling for more. From there, the Thai Martial Artist and I did a combination firebreak. This consisted of two separate stacks of the 12-inch square tiles with gasoline poured on them and ignited.

During the break, which was successful for both of us, the crowd went ballistic. I felt good about the whole situation until I realized my pants were on fire. A Martial Artist saved me with a bucket of water which put me out. It still left a nice size blistered burn on my leg.

I thought I could return to my seat. I waved to the crowd and was about to step out of the ring. One on the Thais asked me, "Do you fight in exhibition bout with one of our kick boxers?"

I said, "No, I've had enough".

The Thai insisted it would only be three rounds one minute each and he said, "It will be fun". He kept saying, "You are very, very, very, good".

I agreed to be in the match and thought to myself, "This can't be that bad".

I sat in one corner of the ring. The Thais wrapped my hands, and took off my sneakers and socks. I looked across the ring to see a heavy-set Thai martial artist getting ready to do battle with me. At first, he did not look that tough. I was soon to find out differently.

After the first round was over, the one-minute seem like on hour. The Thai's kicks had my left eye almost completely shut. He also kicked me repeatedly behind my thigh. I began to badly limp and wondered if I would still be able to walk after the match.

As round two approached, the Thai outside the ring, who now acted the part of coach, kept saying to me, "You must kick behind leg. You must kick behind leg".

They gave me a drink of water and the bell rang for the beginning of round two. All I could hear is Danny in the background screaming, "Zoo, beat his fuckin' head in. Come on, get him, Zoo".

As round two started, I knew I was in for more than an exhibition. In fact, I was the exhibition. As my opponent repeatedly kicked me behind the legs and along my face, he seemed to become faster and faster with his hands and feet. I felt like I was fighting a fly that buzzes around but never lands.

At the end of round two, I could definitely feel the effects of cigarettes and beer as I dragged my sorry ass to the corner. I sat down in the chair. My coach wiped my face. He kept saying to me, "You must kick behind leg. You must kick behind leg. You are going to get yourself hurt".

I was already hurt and I could not take the coach's advice and kick behind my opponent's leg because I could not lift my leg to kick. I could barely walk. I thought to myself, "You crazy, stupid, bastard, getting yourself involved in this. I am here for R & R. It's going to take me a month to recuperate if this keeps up".

I knew I only had one minute and I was still conscious and able to deliver a blow or two. As round three began, I tried to cover my thighs the best that I could to prevent my adversary from doing any more damage. That is exactly what the Thai wanted me to do.

As I would lower my hands to block his feet, it left my upper body open and he would start pounding away at my face. At one point, I blocked one of his punches and landed a huge over right that knocked the Thai right on his butt. At first, I did not think he was going to get up, but he did. We finished off the third round with a flurry of punches back and forth. The bell rang. I went to shake hands and he bowed to me and then shook my hand.

I would not say I won the fight, but I could not wait to get out of the ring so I could have another cold beer. The spectators started buying me beers, too. As I sat down in the bleachers, I found that the workout the Thai gave me was really starting to tell on my body.

I finally had to return to the Hotel room and lay down, so I could heal a little bit from the kickboxing incident.

After a several hour nap and a nice warm bath, Danny and I were ready to go out on the town again. Danny said, "Let's go back to the kick boxing area". There was still the zoo that he wanted to see. I agreed and off we went.

Though I was still a little bit sore, I was still happy to be away from the jungles of Vietnam. When we arrived at the zoo, we saw numerous small cages measuring three feet high and four feet wide.

As we got closer, I noticed a small pond (about thirty feet in diameter) filled with grey, murky water. I noticed a bamboo pole sticking up four feet in the air in the middle of the pond. There was a board attached to the pole with wire. It said caution keep away in big red letters.

I said to Danny, "I wonder what the hell this is". He said, "It might be Alligators". I said, "I don't think so. Let's go check it out anyway". As we got closer I heard a voice behind me said, "GI, don't go near. Very dangerous if you fall in".

I looked at him. He held a big bucket in his right hand, a long Bamboo pole in his left hand, and had a smile on his face.

He said, "Don't get any closer. Very dangerous, man eating Catfish".

I looked at Danny and said, "You gotta be fucking kidding me. There ain't no such thing as a man eating Catfish".

The little Thai man took a long pole and tapped on the short pole that stuck up in the middle of the pond. The gray pond erupted with what seemed like millions of Catfish. They intertwined themselves, like snakes. At this point Danny said, "It must be feeding time". The Thai threw a bucket of chum into the murky waters. The fish immediately devoured the food.

I wondered to myself why they did not have this pond fenced in. There was no doubt in my mind that if you accidentally fell in you were not coming out alive.

I looked at Danny and said, "I have seen enough of this. Let's go see what's in those cages". As we got closer, I saw signs that read "Caution". There were ten cages containing venomous and non-venomous snakes.

I was looking at one when Danny yelled out, "Hey, Zoo, come and look at the size of this snake".

I walked over to the cage. It happened to be a huge Boa Constrictor. It was almost as big as an Anaconda, with a head the size of an NFL Football. It probably measured around 25 inches. It was peacefully asleep in its cage.

Danny pulled a joint from his pocket and lit up. As I walked along the cages, looking at the other snakes, Danny yelled, "Hey, Zoo, how about if I pull about ten feet of this Boa Constrictor out of its cage and you take a picture of me holding the Boa around my neck. Then, I'll give it to you and I'll take your picture holding it"

I said, "No thanks, you're out of your fucking mind if you think I am going to do that. I will take the picture. But I strongly suggest you leave it alone".

Danny opened the cage door any way. He reached in, and grabbed the Boa by the head. He had a hard time getting it out of the cage because of its size. It appeared to be still sleeping. Out it came, a foot at a time, until there was enough of the snake draped around Danny's neck to take a photo.

Danny struggled with the weight of the snake and yelled, "Hey, Zoo, hurry up and take the picture. This thing is heavy". I was about to snap the picture when the light from Danny's Mary Jane cigarette fell off and landed on the snake's head. Immediately, the snake's eyes opened. In an instant, the Boa was constricting around Danny's neck. He started screaming, "Help, get it off of me" while the huge monster wrapped itself several more times around Danny's body.

At first, I did not know what to do. I ran to him, grabbed the snake's big head and started trying to pull it off Danny. It was like trying to hold onto a greased pig. Then the snake's digestive system, which is two to three feet behind the mouth, blew a shit storm all over Danny and me.

*Danny wrestled a Boa like this from its cage.*

I started screaming for help. The situation was way out of control and Danny was going unconscious from the snake's grip on him. Several Zoo Keepers came running. They pried the snake loose with sticks, all the while, yelling at Danny in Thai. They were very angry with him for messing with the snake.

After several minutes, they got the snake off Danny and back into its cage. An ambulance had to take Danny to Don Muang Air Force Base hospital in Bangkok. He had some major bruising and several broken ribs. They kept him for a couple days in the hospital. He never told anyone a Boa Constrictor attacked him at a zoo.

# The Tiger Shark

I knew that our R & R was over in a couple of days. I returned to the hospital with Danny's belongings and left them there for him. I wondered what do to do with myself for the next two days. I talked to several people who had been to Thailand on R&R more than once. They told me that the Gulf of Siam was a nice place to visit and quiet and peaceful. My guide told me he knew just the place and asked me if I wanted some female companionship to go with.

At first, I worried because of VD. Many of my friends in Vietnam came down with the clap. It would be nice to have company, however, so the guide took me to a place where the shops featured women as merchandise.

I looked around and picked out four women, out of fifteen, that I wanted to take with me. I asked the Guide to go make a deal, with whoever was in charge. The girls each had a number attached to their shirt or dress. I guess it was easier than calling them by name.

The Madam did not want to let four of her girls go out to the Gulf of Siam with me. She relented after I convinced her I would take good care of them and get them back safe. I also pointed out that the Guide would be with us.

The six of us left in a small open sided bus propelled by a motorcycle attached to the front. We stopped for beer and cigarettes and away we went.

The trip lasted an hour. We arrived at a small lagoon with Palm Trees and four vacant huts. I thought, "This is beautiful".

Then I remembered that I forgot to buy food. The girls were resourceful, however. One of them said, "Chop, Chop?" (This meant food). One girl had some rice; two others disappeared and returned in a half hour with bananas and coconuts. I asked one of the girls, "How are we going to open theses coconuts?"

She goes, "No problem, got big knife". She reached into her purse and pulled out a half moon machete that was razor sharp.

I lay inside the hut and looked out at the lagoon. I enjoyed a joint while sipping on coconut milk and getting a back rub.

Suddenly, out of nowhere came a small motorboat. It pulled up to the shore in front of our party. The man on the boat wanted to know if I wanted to go water skiing for a price, of course. I was unsure if the boat had enough power to pull me out of the water. Nevertheless, I agreed to try it. I waded into the water and got the skis on. Then I gave him the okay to go. He had the throttle wide open, but I knew he did not have enough power to lift me out of the water.

All of a sudden the boat stopped. I figured the boat driver realized that he could not pull me. I took off the skis. The water was about five feet deep where I stood. Then I see the boat headed back towards me very fast. The driver was waving his arms and yelling something. I could not hear him. As the boat got closer, I wondered why he was not slowing down. I thought he was going to try to kill me with the boat. He slammed the boat in reverse along side of me and started screaming and pulling my arm, "Get in boat, get in boat".

I got in the boat with the assistance of the boat driver who used various means of pulling me into the vessel. He yanked me by the hair, and then he started hauling me into the boat by jerking on my arm and then my bathing suit. I finally entered the boat face first. I had some damage to my face; my arm hurt like hell, and the wedgie the boat driver gave me when he yanked my bathing suit was not feeling too good either. I was really pissed off and looked up at him from the floor of the boat, and yelled, "What the fuck's the matter with you?"

His eyes were bulging out of his head. When a big thump hit the boat, it almost knocked him over. He looked at me and said, "Tiger Shark, very bad".

"I said what?" Then I looked over the side of the boat and saw a dorsal fin running along side the boat. It was about two feet out of the water. I thought my heart was going to stop as I saw how huge the shark was as it swam away from us. If it was not for the boat driver, I am sure I would have been that predator's lunch.

I returned to shore. The girls were horrified because they saw the shark from where they stood.

After they calmed down, I asked them where I could wash the salt off my skin. They said there was no clean water here. With that, I returned to the little hut, drank all the beer and Rice wine, and had some more pot and sex. We partied into the night until I passed out.

*A Tiger Shark almost ate Zoo for lunch.*

In the morning, my breakfast consisted of bananas and coconut milk. I was anxious to get back to somewhere and wash the salt of my body. We left our little Paradise. I asked the Guide to drop me off at the Air Force Base, so I could go visit Danny, then take the girls back and return for me in about an hour.

When I reached the Air Force Base, I was tired, hung over and smelled raunchy. I managed to get a shower in the hospital. I visited Danny. He worried about what would happen if he did not come back to Vietnam with me. I assured him I would explain his accident and his whereabouts to his Company Commander.

Although, I figured his Commander already knew he was injured and in the hospital.

I left the hospital and went to the airport. There I waited for my flight back to Cam Rahn Bay, Vietnam. Overall, my R & R did not seem that restful, but it was good to get out of Nam for a while.

# Enemy Buildup

Upon my return from R & R in Thailand, Alpha Company geared up for an operation. They were near where the Crescent Valley meets the Tiger Mountains. There was a build up of enemy activity in these areas. Alpha Company $2^{nd}$ Platoon was the lead element into the area of operation. The rest of the Company was to follow behind.

Once we arrived at the base of the Tiger Mountains, all the leaders discovered the Choppers put us down in the wrong place. We had to get out of sight before the enemy spotted us. The leaders found out what was going on and learned that we were within walking distance of our correct location.

Many of the men were pissed off because of an extra mile they had to walk with a heavy rucksack. We walked for about an hour, taking short breaks until we sat down for lunch under the thick jungle canopy. I went right to my favorite food: peaches, pound cake, beans, and franks. I always ate dessert first before someone else spotted it.

While I ate, I looked up to see Gary coming over. He sat down by me. He looked at me and said, "Hey, Zoo, how was R & R?"

I replied, "I had a real exciting time, but I'll have to tell you later on when we have more time to talk".

His eyes got as big as half dollars and he said, "Hey, man, did you ever hear of the "Mad Thumper?"

I looked at him and said, "Who the fuck is the Mad Thumper?"

Gary said, "He's some big NVA or Viet Cong whose been going around with an M79 grenade launcher, following various American patrols and waiting for them to take a break. Then at will he would fire five or six rounds up in the air to land close to where they rested.

By the time the grenades exploded, he would vanish. He was a nuisance and caused a lot of damage. (Note: The Mad Thumper would fire one or two rounds just before dark, and always hit someone. After some time, Robert finally laid out for him one night and killed him. This was after he took out thirty or forty soldiers. His M79 Grenade Launcher was brand new and so was the ammo).

Gary kept asking me, "Did you know, Zoo, that we're fuckin' surrounded?" I looked at him and said, "Who gives a fuck. We'll get out of this place, don't worry about it". With that Gary said, "Fuckin' A". Then, he returned to his rucksack.

The Lieutenant said, "We will stay here for the evening". It was around 4:00 P.M. and getting very foggy. Rain drizzled onto the jungle canopy. I wanted to write a letter home but could not find anything dry to use. Therefore, I lay under my poncho in the rain and thought about the "Mad Thumper". I was curious why everyone was so worried about him.

"Why don't they just go out and kill the bastard?" I wondered.

A wet dawn finally arrived. The Lieutenant said, "C'mon guys, let's get it on. We have a long way to go".

I was thinking to myself that my R&R was too short. Now I am back doing the same shit. It seemed, on this particular day, to be the hottest one I ever experienced in Vietnam. About every half-hour, the men were exhausted from the terrain, the extreme humidity, and their heavy rucksacks. The temperature was in the low hundreds. The deep jungle canopy as cover was no respite from the unbearable heat. Eventually all things came to a halt. Exhaustion affected everyone, even the Lieutenant. He said, "That's all for today. I don't care, we aren't going any farther".

When I thought about it, it seemed that the war stopped. I knew the enemy had to be feeling the heat just like us. Everything was quiet all around us until 2:00 AM. Then all hell broke loose in the 2nd Platoon.

We were not sure at that moment what the hell was going on, but there were tracers and explosions not too far from where our Platoon was situated. (A tracer round is ammunition that is chemically treated to glow so you can follow its flight).

Everybody got their gear and weapons and was eager to join the fight. We waited for Orders from the Lieutenant as to our plan of attack.

We made our way slowly through the jungle in the direction of the 2$^{nd}$ Platoon. It was pretty much feel your way through, as it was dark with no Moon. We hoped to avoid any land mines or booby traps. The orders for me and four other men were to go in an upward direction and the others were to go downward.

The firing ceased, as we got closer. It was calm for about an hour. Then the fear and anxiety level rose to a peak once again. As we approached the position, I could hear something in the distance like a clicking noise. As I got closer, I thought it sounded very familiar, but I still could not place the sound. When I got even closer and listened, it dawned on me the noise was coming from a P38 can opener (Army Issue).

I crept up until I was one inch from the head of the soldier that was making the noise. When I tapped him on the shoulder, he almost had a heart attack right there. He said, "Who the fuck are you, man?"

I said, "I'm Doc Zoo and we are here to back you up". By then, the enemy disappeared and it was becoming daylight. It seemed to be one big cluster fuck because there were 2$^{nd}$ and 3$^{rd}$ Platoons in the same area. At this point, the two Platoons went their separate ways to avoid detection by the enemy. About a half hour later, the enemy re-engaged the 3rd Platoon.

Daylight made it easier to go to the 3rd Platoon's aid. However, we still had to avoid booby traps and land mines. The enemy started using a mortar attack against the 3rd Platoon and they took many casualties. At one point, the Company Commander took the full force of a mortar round. It instantly killed him.

When my Platoon got to the 3rd's location, Gun ships were in the air and there were many wounded. I helped with the wounded and did as much as I could to assist the other Medic. By then, more reinforcements arrived and the fight seemed to be over for the time being.

Once again, the two Platoons went different ways in search of the enemy. Then, some good news came. Command ordered an extraction back to LZ Uplift for a three-day stand down. We were all joyful to get out of that hellhole even for a little while.

We returned to LZ Uplift and I went back to Company B Medical. My favorite person, Staff Sergeant Ray, greeted me. He proudly boasted to me, "I see the sorry mother fucker made it through another one".

He walked up to me as I was setting my gear outside my Hooch. I privately wondered what he wanted me to do now.

*Zoo taking a break outside CO B Medical Aid Station at LZ Uplift.*

    He put his arm around me and said, "Come here cat with nine lives, I want to talk to you". He said some Captain wanted to see me and he was not sure what he wanted. He gave me directions to where I had to go to see this person. He even told me, "You don't have to go now. Take a shower and get something to eat. Just see him before the end of the day".

    I thought I was in trouble so I went immediately. As I entered the tent, I saluted to the Captain and said, "Specialist Costigan reporting as ordered, Sir".

    He returned my salute, told me, "at ease and sit down". He kind of smiled and handed me several papers stapled together. He said, "Congratulations on your promotion, Sergeant".

I did not realize that I scored second highest in points (accumulated for doing a good job) in the whole Battalion. The Captain asked me what were my plans when I return to the States. I did not realize it, but my tour of duty was up and I was soon to be going back home. I had an option to extend my tour of duty for six months. I could get an early out of the Army and get a thirty-day leave to go home.

I figured, well I made it this far, and I really did not want to leave the people that I was with, so I accepted another tour.

I arrived back in the United States on January 2, 1970. For the most part, I was weary from the long travel. As I stepped onto the tarmac from the plane, I saw my parents anxiously waiting for me. They had their faces pinned against the waiting area window.

It seemed like a lifetime that I was gone. We stopped to have a few drinks in one of the airport bars. I told them I signed up for one more tour in Nam. They were horrified to hear me say that. They thought I was home for good. To please my Mom, I told her I would be working in the Aid Station. My father took me aside later and simply said, "Aid Station, my ass!"

I did not want to alarm my parents. I talked about Vietnam as little as possible. However, I did have them sold on the idea of my making the military a career and becoming a medical doctor.

I lounged around for a couple weeks. I saw a few friends and then I headed back to Nam. Travel ate six days of my leave.

When I returned to Company B Medical, the Helicopter no sooner landed than I heard, "Speaking of it, there's the sorry mother fucker now!" Staff Sergeant Ray was glad to see me, then the smile faded from his face. He said, "Your boys are in deep shit out there, Zoo. Man, are they ever going to be glad to see you".

Alpha Company was shorthanded due to a lot of wounded men, soldier's tours ending and them going home, and men going on R & R. Command shuffled a few people from different Platoons around and a few soldiers from 3$^{rd}$ Platoon, along with myself, were now in 2$^{nd}$ Platoon. Even with the shuffling around of personnel, we still only had a dozen men in the Platoon (Platoons, in the jungle, usually consisted of about 25 men. The normal compliment of a Platoon is one officer and forty-four men.).

When I arrived in the field, I found that I knew most of the men in 2nd Platoon. The men that I did not know knew of me. They seemed glad I was their Medic.

Once we were out in the jungle, I introduced myself to the men I did not know, as Doc Zoo. I told them that if they needed anything to feel free to ask me. I also told them, "Please do not yell Medic when we are in a fire fight. Just yell Zoo and I will be there".

I insisted that everyone call me Zoo out in the field. Someone yelling Medic makes me a target for the NVA/Viet Cong. Medics and Radio Men are their favorite people to shoot. In addition, the NVA could yell Medic, also. In the midst of a firefight, I would not know who was yelling.

After a couple of days, I knew everyone. They were all hard-nosed characters that could handle anything that came their way. One of my most favorite soldiers I met was Reb. He was 6' 2" and very lanky. His could stare a hole in you with his eyes. He looked like he would murder anyone that crossed his path. He was our point man. He asked me, in a Virginia drawl, "Can you fix this cut I have here on my arm?"

I said, "Sure, not a problem". I began to clean the wound and bandage it.

While I was fixing his arm, I noticed he had several knives in holders, hanging from various parts of his body.

I remarked to him, "I guess you like knives, huh?"

He brought his head down level with mine, flipped a button on his web gear, and grabbed a knife. (Web gear carries canteens, bandages, grenades, and smoke grenades for half-day mission or patrol. It is smaller than a rucksack).

In a continuous movement, he winged the knife. It stuck in a tree about ten feet away. He had speed, precision, and accuracy. He looked at me and finally got back to my yet unanswered question.

He simply said, "Yea, I do".

As time went on, Reb and I became very good friends. One day I asked him, "Hey, Reb, how about teaching me how to throw a knife?" He agreed.

From then on, every chance we had, Reb taught me how to knife throw. After a few months, I started to become proficient.

One day as we were sitting in a clump of trees taking a break, we got the news that a new Lieutenant was joining our Platoon. We were not sure who he was, but we hoped he was not a Cherry Lieutenant.

Whatever or whoever he was, we had to wait for him to arrive before we could judge for ourselves.

Most of the Platoon was seasoned veterans. However, they would be willing to help the Lieutenant out if he were new in country. As he we sat under the trees, we heard news that the new Lieutenant was coming from our Mortar Platoon.

After a couple minutes I said, "Wait a minute guys, this could be a blessing in disguise. He's probably a forward observer and if he can send mortars out to hit the enemy, I'm sure he can call it in with the same accuracy". Map reading is crucial in calling in air strikes or artillery.

When he arrived, the new Lieutenant seemed quiet at first. He introduced himself and told us not to call him Lieutenant in the field. Most of the Platoon called him Sir or Lieutenant Ed. It did not take long before all of us grew to like him. Even to this day, his Platoon members still keep in touch with him.

He was soft spoken, but had full charge of his leadership. The Platoon really respected Lieutenant Ed. We were soon to learn that under tense situations, Lieutenant Ed always had a plan, a back-up plan, and a plan for the back-up plan, in case something went wrong.

He was the only man that I knew that could have a conversation on the radio while on a dead ass run, calling out firing coordinates.

# The Hawk's Nest And The Ledge

There was an enemy buildup and Command had us running all over the place looking for the NVA/Viet Cong. One day, Command told us to take a break. They explained a plan to extract us from the jungle and put us down in a village near the ocean.

The Navy needed some security for one of their munitions barges that broke loose. It rested on a sandbar in the South China Sea. It was not too far from shore, and Command was determined not to let the enemy get near it. As I was standing on the beach, watching the Navy Divers from a distance, out of nowhere came a submarine. It breached like a whale. It was only 400 yards from the beach.

After it surfaced, thirty men stood on the deck, fully armed. They guarded the munitions barge as the Navy Divers worked to free it from the sandbar.

*Looking East from top of Hawk Mountain to South China Sea.*

We were there from morning until late afternoon. Then we had the hike of our lives. I asked one soldier, "Where the fuck are we going, now?" as we disappeared into the thick jungle. He said, "We're going to the Hawk's Nest, Zoo. Haven't you ever been there before?"

I answered, "negative", but I later found out that the climb could make a mountain goat drag his nuts; by the time it reached the top.

At least we had the opportunity to rest while guarding the barge. There was no resting this time. By the time we got to the top of the Hawk's Nest, I was fucking exhausted and angry. It was a very steep mountain; the way up was a zigzag path cut into the dirt. The path was narrow, only wide enough for one person, and dangerously steep. I carried a full rucksack and it seemed like it must be the stairway to heaven.

When we arrived at the summit, it was dark. I was eager to get some sleep. I asked the Lieutenant, "What about guard duty?"

The other men laughed and said, "No body is going to come up here. Get some rest".

The next day when I awoke, the view amazed me. Looking out to the east was the South China Sea. Looking south would be the Valleys below. West and north was the Tiger Mountains.

*Top of Hawk's Nest, looking southeast towards the Hoa Tan Villages.*

The Hawk's Nest was about three-fourths the size of a football field in circumference. It had rows and rows of barbed wire and one entrance. It consisted of a radio shack, a helipad, five rows of concertina wire, and a toilet dug in the ground. From the other angles, it was impossible to infiltrate by land navigation. An experienced mountain climber would find it virtually impossible to get pass the perimeter.

We looked for the enemy located between the Hawk's Nest and the stranded barge. We never did have a chance to engage them. The enemy would never be able to get to the Hawk's Nest to attack us because it is almost impossible to get up there. If they did get up there, our jets would blast them right off the face of the mountain, anyway.

*Bong Song pass, Highway 1.*

Our scenic tour ended the next day when Command ordered us extracted to another location. It just seemed the more we looked for the NVA/Viet Cong the less we saw of them. Nevertheless, Lieutenant Ed reminded us to keep a sharp eye out; that we were still in enemy territory.

*American Soldiers also called the Bong Song Pass V.C. Valley.*

We were in the lower Crescent Valley for about three weeks. We wanted to return to LZ Uplift for a stand-down. Everyone was near exhaustion. Instead, Command transferred us near Delta Company's area of operations. Intelligence and aerial reports spotted numerous enemy activities around the area.

It was towards the end of March when we set up an ambush in anticipation that the NVA/Viet Cong would come our way. This was because they were trying to infiltrate into Delta Company's area of operations. No one was sure how many enemy soldiers were around us. We were ready for the worst. We found an old NVA Outpost that was right at the mouth of a hidden trail. We set up the ambush there.

It was just getting dark when about 25-40 enemy soldiers walked into the back of our ambush sight. Jim reacted immediately and shot one of the NVA soldiers.

Suddenly, we found ourselves surrounded. Then the shit hit the fan. Bullets flew all around our position. Then we started running out of ammo.

Our Squad Leader spotted a rock ledge right near the ambush sight. We all ran for the sight and ducked under the ledge. I was pinned in between Paul and Pat. We were down to pistols and knives and determined that we are not going to give up. Surrender was out of the question.

Fortunately, the NVA/Viet Cong did not have scout dogs with them or they would have found us hiding under the ledge. If they looked down, they would have found us. They were three feet away from us. The ledge that we hid under had half the NVA/Viet Cong standing on it above us. The dirt from the boots of one of the NVA/Viet Cong hit me on the face and nose. If I stuck my hand out, I could have touched his toes. That is how close they were. The tension was thick. We held our breath in unison. Besides the enemy over our heads, we had a FNG (Fucking New Guy) with us. He was starting to panic.

Mike tried to calm him down and keep him quiet so the enemy did not hear him. He had his hand over his mouth. The FNG looked at me. I pulled my knife and motioned to him that I would slit his throat if he made a sound.

This was one of the scariest fucking moments of my life. If the FNG made a sound we were all dead.

The NVA got diverted to another area, since they couldn't find us there, so we seized the window of opportunity and got the fuck out of there.

We started to run and when we broke into a clearing by a rice paddy the enemy spotted us. We turned around and used the last of our ammo for our last stand. It held the enemy off for a brief time and broke their ranks.

That gave us enough time, once again, to get a slight lead on them. They chased us for about 2000 meters along a main trail. When we came to a streambed, Mike and I fell behind to cover the withdrawal of the rest of the Platoon.

Mike and I were down to only a few grenades. We waited until the enemy ran up on us. At the right time, I threw a baseball grenade (M-33). Mike winged a white Phosphorus grenade. (When phosphorus hits the skin, it continues burning. You cannot put it out with water. Smothering the wound is the best method. Mud effectively seals off the wound. Otherwise, the phosphorus continues burning until it exits your body).

The Phosphorus grenade stopped the enemy for only a moment. Suddenly, the FNG appears out of nowhere and runs right into the explosion of the phosphorus grenade. Unfortunately, he was also running towards the enemy.

The FNG started screaming. I had to rescue his ass. I tackled him and threw him in the stream to see if any phosphorus hit him. (I gave him a fast douse to see if he bubbled). I determined that he was more confused and scared than injured. Then I laughed to myself because I was petrified and horrified at that point, also. He was not the only one scared shitless.

I got him on his feet. I kept yelling at him to, "C'mon you're alright". I finally threw him over my shoulder and Mike and I started running to where the rest of the Platoon was. By that time, a Platoon from Delta Company was out there to help us. We were able to make it into the Command Post without further fighting.

If I had a fifth of Jack Daniels I would have immediately chugged the whole bottle to calm my nerves. We out fought and out smarted the enemy in every way. The NVA/Viet Cong definitely licked their wounds that day. We had no casualties. While we were in Delta Company's Command Post, it was my first introduction to some of the men from Delta Company.

One in particular was Robert. He was bitching and screaming about the NVA/Viet Cong. I sensed that he did not like these people. I introduced myself to him as Zoo, the Medic.

He said, "Yea man, I know you. You are the crazy fucker that makes all the animal cries at night in the jungle".

I said, "Yea, it scares hell out of the enemy. Keeps them wondering what is going on. "I knew Robert for several months before I found out that Command awarded him the Soldier's Medal."

He exhibited extraordinary bravery in saving the lives of some local villagers. It is the highest award given for heroism in a non-Combat situation.

# Chieu Hoi Program

The Republic of Vietnam Government developed an amnesty program, called "Open Arms", for the benefit of the North Vietnamese Army and the Viet Cong.

Designed to give the enemy an opportunity to surrender, the program included a drop of thousands of leaflets in the jungles and rice patties directed at the North Vietnamese Army and the Viet Cong. The leaflet promised much better treatment than they were getting from their own people.

I once saw a North Vietnamese Officer all spit shined and uniform pressed with his hands behind his head taken prisoner by the Americans. He actually spent three days looking for the American soldiers, because of hunger and thirst.

His main motivation for seeking out the American soldiers, however, was because he received word that the North Vietnamese Army killed his family. He also spoke English, and wanted to get even with the NVA for the murder of his family. I watched as soldiers escorted the prisoner to a Helicopter while under guard.

Two months later, I saw the prisoner again. He returned and began working with the 173rd Airborne as a "Kit Carson Scout".

*Doc Zoo attends to the sick in the Village of Van Cam. An RVN soldier accompanies him as part of the Civil Action Program.*

The Scouts, once forced to fight for the North Vietnamese Army, were glad to have an opportunity to work with the Americans. They gladly accepted this idea. These "Scouts" proved to be valuable, as they knew where to look for the North Vietnamese Army and the Viet Cong. They could also interrogate the enemy in their own language and then translate.

Unfortunately, the North Vietnamese soldier only lived about three weeks as a "Scout" before he died in a battle with the North Vietnamese Army.

# Five Fngs
## July 1969

---

Gerry told me (Zoo) this story of his first day in 2nd Platoon with five other FNGs. They took a Huey from LZ Uplift to the east end of the Crescent Valley. They landed around 8:00 A.M at the edge of a rice paddy. It was Alpha Company's re-supply day, the most exciting time you can have in the field. The soldiers hurriedly unloaded the provisions, which often included mail and clothes.

Sometimes care packages arrived from home. The men often shared the contents with the other soldiers. Thomas was the one responsible for getting our mail and packages to us out in the jungle. He did a good job and we appreciated his efforts. Paratroopers directed the FNGs to hide in the tree line when they finished unloading.

There was a dozen or so rough looking Paratroopers, sitting around in different areas. They did not pay attention to the five Fucking New Guys. We sat down and waited. Gerry said it was hot as hell and he sweated like a Polar Bear in the tropics.

About ten minutes later, after the soldiers unloaded it, the Chopper lifted off. A soldier introduced himself to Gerry as Staff Sergeant Harry. Gerry did not know his rank for sure because he did not wear any Sergeant Stripes.

He looked at him and said, "What the fuck am I gonna do with a little Mother Fucker like you?" At 5'4", Gerry did not tower over other people.

The Sergeant continued to Gerry, "You're too damn small to hump an M-60, and too small to hump the radio. I am going to make a Point Man out of you. Good luck!" Then he walked away.

Gerry said that the other FNGs just looked at him and shook their heads. Solis was the only one to tell Gerry, "Don't worry, man. You will be okay". Then he smiled. Solis and Gerry remained close friends until Solis was killed on January 7, 1970.

He said the five new FNGs had to endure the other Paratroopers crap when they started messing with them and calling them cherries and shit like that. The Paratroopers said, "Man, what did you do to piss off Uncle Sam enough to get your ass sent to the Nam?"

It was now 10:30 A.M, but the harassment continued. Sergeant Harry finally called to Gerry, "Get your shit and come with me".

They walked over to four men with their web gear on. They all carried an M-16. Harry says, "This Is Gerry. He is on patrol. He will walk slack for Bobby". (Slack is the second man back on a patrol, directly behind the point man).

Gerry said a 2$^{nd}$ Lieutenant named Suspy led the Patrol. He said you could not tell he wore stripes and that he looked sloppy. He also had on enlisted man's fatigues. Gerry figured he did not want any of the enemy mistaking him for an Officer and shooting him. Any way, Gerry said that Lieutenant Suspy was a stand-in until his Platoon could get a replacement.

Bobby, the Point Man, (he was a Green Beret) assured Gerry not to be nervous. He told him, "This is a routine patrol. We're just going to this Village to see if we can get information about Viet Cong who come in at night to get food".

Bobby further warned Gerry, "If we hit any shit, you better cover my ass. Lay down as much fire as you can".

The Lieutenant had a Radio Operator by the name of Will. He and Gerry eventually became close friends. Gerry described Will as mellow as fine wine and said he never panicked. He said the other member of the Patrol was Char. He walked drag.

Gerry explained that Sergeant Harry instructed him as to what kind of supplies he needed. "You need twenty-one magazines of ammo and four Frags and a lot of water".

When the Sergeant finished, Lieutenant Suspy yelled, "Let's move out". They began their journey, which would last for three or four hours. In forty minutes, they reached the top of a small hill named "Hill 10".

Gerry said that Lieutenant Suspy called for the Platoon to take a break. They kept their distance from each other. (Sitting together presented one, large, convenient target to the enemy).

Gerry said sweat poured off him as if he was taking a hot, salty shower. He was soaking wet. The temperature at 11:00 A.M. had to be at least 100 degrees under the jungle canopy.

Gerry said a soldier named Fin complained about Gerry's position. It was because Gerry was a FNG. After the complaint, Gerry's position changed from Drag to the rear when they continued their journey.

The Platoon started down "Hill 10". Gerry said that they were twenty meters into their descent when the loudest explosion he ever heard went off. He said the blast blew Fin about ten feet into the air. Lieutenant Suspy fell forward, holding his crotch. Bobby grabbed his ass.

Gerry said he and Will escaped the booby trap, but the noise from the blast seriously compromised Gerry's hearing. He said Will looked at him and told him to check on Fin (they did not have a Medic with them). Will had to resort to hand signals since Gerry could not hear him. Gerry went over to Fin, who was flat on his back.

Gerry said, "Man, was he a mess. He had at least thirty wounds; some holes the size of golf balls".

He said Fin groaned to him, "Am I gonna die?"

Gerry said he finished looking Fin over and told him, "I don't think so. I do not see any wounds to your vital parts". Then Will yelled over to Gerry that The Dustoff (Medevac) is on its way.

Gerry said he used every bandage everyone had and even took his shirt off and tore it into strips to try to patch up Fin. Then Gerry said he had to have a private moment of insanity before the Dustoff (Medevac) arrived.

Finally, the Chopper lands and two Medics jump off with a stretcher. They headed to where Gerry was tending the wounded soldier, picked up Fin, and lay him on the stretcher. Gerry said Will joined them and the four of them started towards the Dustoff (Medevac) with the stretcher.

Gerry said Lieutenant Suspy ran in front of them and tripped one of the Medics. He said they dropped Fin, who screamed with pain when he hit the ground.

Gerry said that Suspy showed no regard for his troops as he tried to get on the Dustoff (Medevac) first. He said that was the last time they saw the man, which was a good thing, since they lost all respect for him.

They finally got Fin on the Chopper. Then the Medics looked at Bobby who was bleeding from his buttocks, but he refused to get on the Chopper. After the Dustoff (Medevac) left, Gerry said Bobby took them back to their Platoon. He said this was another good thing, because Will and Gerry did not know how to get there on their own.

A few days later, Gerry heard the fate of the three paratroopers. Another Dustoff (Medevac) came later and took Bobby to the hospital when they got back to their Platoon. This saved his life because the shrapnel penetrated his intestines.

Lieutenant Suspy lost one of his balls, which seemed fitting to Gerry. Fin lost his right arm and leg.

Gerry explained to Zoo that he went on a couple hundred Recon Patrols and Night Ambushes after that first one and the only injury he received was from a punji stake.

He said, that first Patrol taught him that he had a good chance of never getting out of Vietnam alive. He said, "This was serous shit!" From then on, Gerry said he never let his guard down and that he was very lucky.

Meanwhile, the explosion that sent three men to the hospital still had Gerry's ability to hear screwed up. He said his ears rang all day and into the night. The Platoon humped over to a small base camp that had a couple bunkers, fox holes and trenches all around the perimeter with some layers of barbed wire.

Sergeant Harry assigned Gerry guard duty from midnight to 2:00 A. M. and showed him the location. Gerry said that before his turn for guard duty started, he fell asleep. Sergeant Harry came over to him and kicked him in the side. Gerry jumped up (he says he still remembers the pain). Gerry states that Sergeant Harry started yelling at him, "We are under fire, get your ass on the line".

Incoming green tracers whizzed by Gerry as he ran to the trenches for cover. He had his M-16 and twenty-one magazines. He started firing into the tree line. Even though he could not see anyone, he said he felt he had to keep shooting.

An explosion rocked the compound every ten to fifteen seconds. The "Mad Thumper" was firing his M79 Grenade Launcher at them.

The firefight lasted for about ten minutes, before the Viet Cong left the area. Gerry declared that none of his Platoon was injured or killed. Gerry then explained that Sergeant Harry came over to him and asked him, "How the hell could you sleep through all that noise?"

Gerry told the Sergeant that he was very near deaf because of the noise from the booby-trap that morning. The Sergeant explained to him, "I thought you were dead, that's why I kicked you".

When the Platoon got up the next morning, Gerry felt relieved that he lived through his first day in the bush with the 173rd Airborne Brigade. He looks back now and counts his blessings.

# THE SAPPER PLATOON

As the days went on, we played a big game of "hide and go seek" with the enemy. Well trained, well equipped, and well organized, the NVA/Viet Cong would initiate contact with the Americans only when the tactical situation was favorable for them.

*Our Point Man checks out bridge before Patrol crosses. The Bong Song Bridge was built by the French in 1945.*

Our areas of operations ran near the Crescent Valley, the 506th Valley, the Bong Song Pass, and the Tiger Mountains. LZ Uplift was our Station. There was also a small Landing Zone near LZ Uplift, called Fire Base Solis. We used this occasionally. Fire Base Solis, is named in honor of Sgt. Felix Solis, $2^{nd}$ Squad, $2^{nd}$ Platoon, who died on January 7, 1970.

*CO B Medical, LZ Uplift. Blood Soaked litters from two Americans who died July 4, 1969.*

*Sometimes we would go for days without even seeing an enemy presence. It made looking for them more frustrating. The NVA/Viet Cong operations used detailed planning, tactical surprise, and careful reconnaissance in their assaults. Their care in preparing for operations, however, was often their greatest weakness. They were unable to modify their plans to meet new contingencies.*

*Their favorite tactic was the ambush, characterized by a short, violent action followed by a rapid withdrawal. Their other favorites were Sapper attacks (a Viet Cong or NVA solder who gets inside the perimeter, armed with explosives) and harassing operations. They used Sapper attacks to sabotage Military and Governmental Installations, collect intelligence, and terrorize friendly troops.*

*I remember one night, when I had my first encounter with a Sapper Platoon. It was around 7:30 P.M. We were resting at Fire Base Solis for the evening, to get ready for a Mission the next day.*

*Landing at Fire Base Solis after a mission.*

We sent out a night ambush Platoon. It consisted of five or six men. They put out trip wires around the perimeter of the LZ and stationed themselves about 150 feet from the perimeter. They would get in the jungle before dark to detect any enemy intrusion. (A trip wire, used to alert the approach of the enemy, triggers a ground flare).

I would sometimes go out on night ambush, but tonight it was a rainy, nasty night and I was dog assed tired and wanted to get some rest. I was inside of one of the bunkers and just about asleep when all hell broke loose. You could hear bullets coming from every direction.

I came out of the bunker and saw red and white tracers coming from opposite directions. The red ones were ours, and the white ones belonged to the enemy. As it turned out, a superior force of NVA Sappers had surrounded the ambush squad.

Upon hearing the distress call come from the Squad Leader, I grabbed my weapons and medical bags. I knew there had to be dead and wounded Americans on the sight of the firefight. In my haste to get out there, I did not wait for anyone else.

I yelled to somebody to watch the Claymore Mines outside the fence and do not shoot me because I am going out there. Two other Platoon Members tried to restrain me from leaving by myself. I did finally break loose. I ran right into the middle of the firefight yelling, "It's Zoo, don't shoot me".

I heard someone yell, "Zoo, we're over here. Get the fuck out of there, man".

Within a few minutes, the Calvary was right behind me. I stayed near the Point Element of the Platoon's Reactionary Force as they moved towards the surrounded Patrol. I ascertained there were no casualties to friendly troops. I then joined an assault squad that was sweeping the area looking for the enemy.

I noticed something out of the corner of my eye. It was one of the NVA/Viet Cong. He was running to my right about forty yards away from me. As he was running, I was firing in front of him, leading my fire. I knew that I did hit him. He went down, but then got back up. I kept yelling, "They're moving to our right".

What happened next played itself out like a surreal gunfight at the OK Corral. We lined up in a spread out pattern and walked towards the enemy with our guns blasting.

I did not leave sight of the enemy as he ducked into some thick bushes by a small pond. When I arrived seconds later, looking for him, he was already waiting for me. Though wounded, the enemy had plenty of fight left in him.

There was no thought of fear in my mind at that point. I knew I had to win and I did. It was lucky for the night ambush Platoon to have run into the Sapper Platoon. If the Sapper Platoon succeeded in infiltrating the area, they would have done some serious damage to Fire Base Solis.

We went on a few more missions that night with no sign of the enemy. The plan was to return to LZ Uplift for more supplies. However, Command changed those plans and decided to re-supply us in the field. Along with more provisions, we were also getting a few new soldiers (FNGs) as replacements.

At least we had time to take a rest while waiting for our supplies and the FNGs to get here. I wondered to myself what the new guys would be like and had a brief flashback of my first day in the jungle with my rucksack.

# THE TIGER

## July 14, 1970

---

It was a long night of hard rain, and chilling winds. The NVA were on the move near us. We were pulling in a night observation post about twenty-five yards from our camp somewhere in the Tiger Mountains, located in the Central Highlands of Vietnam.

*Ho Chi Minh Trail (rear of picture) in the Central Highlands.*

We took four-hour shifts while the others slept. It was finally morning. Den and I were on guard duty. We felt frozen and hungry and we just wanted to get warm. It was about 5:45 AM. I looked at Den and complained. "Shit, man it's cold out".

"You got that right, Zoo". Den said as he hugged himself to get some heat going in his body.

Though the temperature dropped to the low seventies during the night, it felt like thirty degrees in the jungle. Our day was just beginning and I already felt weary.

I said to Den, "We're going to have to go soon and get ready for the long day ahead of us". I was eager to give sick call and get the men rolling. In particular, a soldier named Doug who suffered from jungle rot and bad infected boils needed attention on a daily basis. Though he never complained, I knew his condition was painful. He never once bitched about it, however.

Rays of light began to peek through the jungle canopy. As I moved to get up, we heard movement out in the jungle in front of us. Perhaps it was the wind, but it got our attention. I looked into Den's eyes, and silently pointed in the direction, from where the noise came from. It was about twenty-five to thirty feet away and seemed to be moving closer towards us.

We quietly took the safes off our M-16's as we crouched down. All we could hear was the subtle rustle of jungle vegetation as the thing continued in our direction. The moment became unbearably tense. We felt the hair standing up on the back of our necks. I could swear I heard Den's heart pounding. We were soaked with sweat in the midst of the cool morning.

I slowly stood up. Although we could not see into the jungle, I was sure now that the enemy was very near our camp. I pointed my rifle in the direction of the sound and got ready to shoot.

Suddenly, like a flash of lightning, a huge, furry animal came flying out of the Jungle, over a stand of bushes right, towards us. (Later, when we calmed down, we figured that the NVA movements in the area must have spooked it).

It hit our trip wires attached to flares, and the whole area lit up like a fireworks display for about twenty seconds. It was a large, Southeastern Asian Tiger. It had to weigh more than five hundred pounds. The heavy cat leaped over the brush, intent on escaping the NVA. The flash of the flares left the big cat, Den, and me blind and startled. I could not see the air born cat until he landed on my chest and knocked me to the ground.

*An Asian Tiger landed on Zoo and knocked him down.*

The animal smelled disgusting, like a mixture of feline urine, skunk spray and musk. The flares were out by now. It was just bright enough to see the cat's huge teeth as his massive head hovered over my face. I was petrified. The Tiger sniffed me all over. There was no doubt in my mind that I was going to be breakfast for the big cat.

The Tiger was nervous and spooked. I expected at any second that he would start to dine on me by clawing and chewing me to bits.   Suddenly, I felt something wet and warm. "Oh, shit!" I didn't know if it was the Tiger or if I was pissing my pants.  I then realized that the Tiger was busily urinating all over me.

The beast did not stop until he pissed on me from head to toe. When he was finished, he let out a growl. Then the cat leapt off me, kicked up the soil with his two hind feet like he wanted to bury me, and headed for our camp.

Still lying on the ground, I started to shake with disbelief that I escaped being the Tiger's breakfast. He never put even a scratch on me. I sat up and looked at Den. "Holy shit, did you see that?" I exclaimed.

Den, was incredulous. "Jesus, Zoo, man, yea". He yelled. "Christ, I think I need to smoke a joint".

It seemed that the whole scene with the Tiger did not take more than ten seconds. When the Tiger tripped the flares, it also alerted the rest of our Platoon. They woke up to see a huge Tiger run right past them through the camp. Men started hollering.

Some yelled, "Did you see that?"

I heard the Lieutenant say, "Let's get the hell out of here. This place sucks".

Den and I rejoined the others. Out of mass confusion and laughter, I gave sick call. As usual, I followed my routine of beginning with the last man and working my way to the front. Before we began our day, as Platoon Medic, I checked if any of the men had any medical difficulties. I especially made sure everyone took his malaria pill.

The sun was up by now. Though it was still early morning, the jungle already felt like a sauna. It grew hotter and steamier as I made my rounds among the men.

Sweat was pouring from my head and burning my eyes. I thought to myself, "Welcome to the jungle".

By the time I set my medical rucksack down next to Doug, my fatigues were soaked with perspiration. Jungle rot infected Doug's shoulder. I began to change his bandage. While I worked, I heard a couple of the men talking.

One of them exclaimed, "Christ, what the hell smells so bad?"

Another said, "Jesus, Mary and Joseph, it's you, Zoo. You smell horrible".

It seems that the heat and humidity effectively raised the smell of Tiger piss on my fatigues to the hundredth power. I was so intent on getting my medical stuff done, that I didn't notice how bad I smelled until someone brought it to my attention. No one would come near me. Nor, could I stand myself. I could hardly breathe from the stench.

One of my Platoon members said to me, "Hey Doc? How about you pulling rear security and stay downwind from us?"

I could not blame them. The smell was so horrible that I do not even think the Viet Cong would come near us.

I said, "I'll walk rear security if you want, but that's not going to happen. The Lieutenant always wants me in the middle".

The Lieutenant yelled, "Okay, hurry up and grab something to eat quickly and get your possessions ready. We'll be moving out shortly".

We had about a four-klick (kilometer) hump ahead of us. As the morning grew hotter, we made our way through the jungle. The smell of Tiger piss on my fatigues grew exponentially with the heat.

There was nowhere to bathe and the little water left in my canteen would never go far enough. When I realized I did not have clean fatigues to change into, I got very depressed. The odor of Tiger piss hung over the Platoon like a smothering gas cloud as we trekked through the jungle. Finally, one of the Squad Leaders made a suggestion to the Lieutenant.

"We got to find some water and get Zoo a bath. The smell is killing us".

The Lieutenant heartily agreed and stopped to consult his map. He saw a small stream not far ahead.

"Zoo, you will get your bath, the Lieutenant promised". He tried not to breathe in while talking to his stinky Medic.

"Great, I can wash off this rotten Tiger piss odor. The whole Platoon is sick from the disgusting smell.

One of my Platoon members promised me a clean set of fatigues if I got a chance to get a bath. I was very grateful. We continued our trek for about another hour. The Lieutenant looked at his map again and saw that the stream he had marked on the map was just ahead.

As soon as we got there, I took off my stinking; Tiger pissed on fatigues and buried them so that the Viet Cong or NVA would not find them. I could not wait to get to the creek with a bar of soap and wash the rotten smell of cat urine off my body. I also volunteered to fill the canteens and bring them back when I was finished washing.

That was probably one of the best baths I ever had. The water in the creek was cold, but washing off the rotten smell felt like heaven.

While I was down in the creek, the rest of the Platoon decided to grab a quick bite to eat. I finished bathing and put on my clean fatigues. I was just tying my boots when I heard talking. I snuck down the creek bed and peaked around the bend. There were four Viet Cong doing the same thing that I was, washing up and filling canteen.

I found myself immersed in an immediate, extreme adrenalin rush. There was no way that I could yell to my Platoon for assistance with out alerting the Viet Cong to our presence.

I pulled the pin on a grenade and threw it as high as I could in the enemy's direction. By the time the grenade landed, I was in the middle of the creek shooting at the enemy with my M-16. Though I wounded three of them, they managed to get away. I shot the fourth one be he also got away and vanished into the jungle with his fellow soldiers.

When my Platoon heard the grenade explode, then me shooting, they ran to the creek with their weapons. I told them what happened. They waded out to the middle of the creek and joined me. We were back at the OK Corral again.

We put the machine gunner in the middle of the creek and the rest of our Platoon flanked him on both sides. Now there were eight, armed soldiers walking side-by-side, down the creek bed, towards where I last saw the enemy. We came to a halt.

I noticed a small blood trail going up into the jungle. I took it upon myself to follow the spore but had no success. The enemy managed to disappear. I then fired several magazines on full automatic into the jungle in hopes of hitting one of them. After that, my Platoon checked out the area. It seemed quiet.

We came out of the jungle near a rice paddy dike. Suddenly, we spotted one of the Viet Cong running along the dike. He was kind of out of range but I fired over his head using windage and elevation on my rifle in hopes of hitting him. The enemy stopped running and ducked behind a Water Buffalo that was standing in the middle of the rice paddy near a farmer.

I yelled, "I'll get this bastard". Two seconds later I had a LAW Rocket set up and fired it right at the Water Buffalo. It was a direct hit. Needless, to say the Viet Cong and the Water Buffalo instantly met their maker. Their organic parts would now become fertilizer for the rice paddy.

I could hear the farmer, bitching up a storm in Vietnamese because I just blew up his livelihood. This War was as much hell for them as it was for us.

# The Cliff

It was misty, cool, yet, humid. We were on combat patrol and started our daily routine about 5:45 am. Everyone usually awakens and tends to their personal needs. The Lieutenant plans his map and strategy for the upcoming daily struggle with the heat, the jungle, the enemy, and the monsoons. Then we got moving.

As we approached a steep, vertical mountain, we all knew we were in for a long nasty day. The jungle on that mountain was intensely thick to the point that it was easier to fight the enemy than it was the foliage. Every inch of the way, the Elephant grass sliced through our fatigues. Sometimes it cut our flesh because it was so razor sharp.

The struggle was long and very slow. We hacked away with machetes, inch by inch to our destination. At around 9:00 A.M, we came to an approach even more difficult than the one we just negotiated. We began climbing. The path became steeper. We started slipping, sliding, and getting frustrated just trying to carry our heavy volume of munitions as we hiked. We were glad we didn't have our rucksacks to carry. (Note: We were on Combat Patrol and did not carry rucksacks. But I did have my Medical Bag with me).

*One hundred and thirty pound rucksack includes ammo.*

(The rucksacks weighed about 100 pounds on a light day. Each man carried enough ammunition and weapons to fight 100 Viet Cong in an instant.)

I armed myself to the teeth. I not only had the regulation M-16. I carried a 12 gauge sawed-off pump shotgun, 45 sidearm, 38 pocket pistol, 4 knives in assorted lengths, a straight razor and a small meat hook.

We marched on. Travel became more impossible. We constantly slid in the mud. For every three steps forward, we slid two steps backwards. Sergeant Mike yelled back to us that we were almost to the top of the mountain.

Suddenly, I heard a faint cry and turned around to see where Gary was. I looked but he was not behind me. I thought to myself, "Christ, he was right here, a second ago".

I looked all around and then popped my head through the brush that lined the trail. I was surprised to see a shear, high cliff behind the vegetation. I spotted Gary. "Shit, he fell a long way down". I thought.

Before I could move or alert the rest of the Platoon, the weight of my medical bag pushed me forward and I fell over the edge, too. Fortunately, I only fell about fifteen feet and landed on a large, round boulder. I landed on my back. I looked up in the air and felt like every bone in my body was broken.

Mike, Lieutenant Ed, and the rest of the Platoon were quickly coming to my rescue. I was able to move and regain my composure within a few minutes. I looked over the rock down at Gary. I thought to myself, "There is no way he could have survived that fall".

The Platoon climbed down to Gary. He was lying on his back on top of a huge rock that was one in a field of many boulders. He was moaning. I arrived moments later. I checked all of his vital signs and asked, "What hurts?" He complained of his right hip being numb. He had no feeling in his feet.

I was unsure how we were going to get him on a Medevac. At first, I did not want to move him. However, within ten minutes or so he was able to sit up. I understood that Gary was in severe pain and possibly fractured his hip or his right leg.

The Lieutenant and the Sergeant talked about extraction methods. The rest of the Platoon secured our area of operations. Because of where Gary landed, it would be difficult to move him.

This became a very intense situation. We had one seriously injured soldier. The Viet Cong could discover us in this vulnerable position. Calling in a Jungle Penetrator to extract Gary was impractical. The thick jungle and the exposure to the aircraft made that plan too dangerous.

We knew the enemy was close by. All of our internal alarms went off, driving our adrenalin. We needed to get Gary quickly extracted to the Aid Station. We used the trail and made a makeshift cradle with rifles to bring Gary up to the top ledge from which he originally fell. It was a quick rescue. It took us twenty minutes to get him back to the top.

Once that was complete, we decided the Helicopter could not get Gary from there. Okay, so now we had to carry him back down the mountain and find a substantial area to set up a Landing Zone for our Dustoff (Medevac) Helicopter to land.

This also was fun. The rain turned the same mountain we just came up into a mudslide going back down. When we finally reached our destination, we were exhausted, frustrated, and ready to kill anything that walked, moved, or crawled anywhere near us.

The Dustoff (Medevac) finally arrived to carry Gary back to Company B Medical for further evaluation.

Just when we thought the day was almost finished, it just started. The Lieutenant said, "Five minute break, boys, then we have to star humping again. We have to go back up the mountain". We all silently groaned at this command.

"Fuckin' A" was the thought in everyone's mind.

# The Gorilla

We were at a point where some Medics were going home. Some left in body bags. In addition, new Medics were coming in country. There was, however, a shortage of soldiers. For a short time, I was working as the temporary Medic for other Platoons and squads that were without a Doctor.

The Platoon I worked with and mostly stayed with was going back to LZ Uplift Base Camp, on a three-day stand down before the next mission. A radio call came for me from my senior Medical NCO. He asked me if I would stay out for two more days and help another Platoon.

I replied, "No problem. See you in forty-eight hours".

A Huey Assault Helicopter extracted my Platoon and I back to LZ Uplift. The men got off at Uplift and the Huey gave me a ride back to the jungle. I arrived at the foot of a small mountain. A bunch of tired, ratty looking soldiers waited for me after they secured the Landing Zone. I did not know them, but I assured them I would take good care of them. I introduced myself as "Zoo".

*Zoo wears blood stained shirt after three days on Patrol in 50 Valley.*

I got to know each man better as the day went on. A sort of bonding and trust started to grow between us. They knew that I was not just the new Medic. I was out in the jungle for many months before meeting them, and had a lot of experience.

We traveled in a small streambed, heading somewhere northwest of Bong Song. The rocky streambed was moss covered and slippery.

*Bong Song Mountains and Highway 1.*

Travel was very slow. The water attracted poisonous snakes, which presented a constant danger, especially the Bamboo Viper.

The reptile is about a foot and one half inches long and is thin bodied and light green. The venom of this snake is so powerful that it will kill you almost instantly.

(We were told the myth about the "two stepper" when we came in country). If the Bamboo Viper bites you, death occurs within your next two or three steps. This is actually bullshit! You can last up to five or six steps before biting the dust.

The day wore on. We did not see the enemy or any signs of them. We stopped for a break in a friendly area. There were other American Troops in the vicinity.

After our break, we continued to search for a possible NVA outpost along the creek bed.

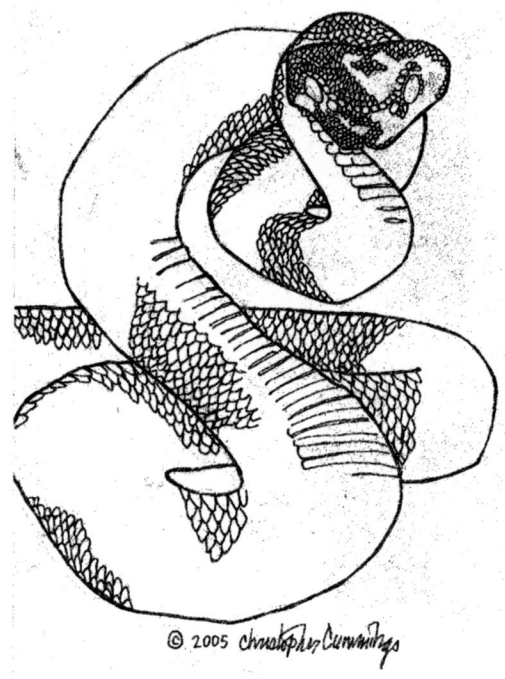

*A deadly Bamboo Viper.*

All of a sudden, our Platoon Leader held up his fist, signaling an immediate stop. I could see the Point Man coming back. He said to the Lieutenant in charge, "You are not going to believe this, but there's a fuckin' Gorilla up there".

The Lieutenant said, "Ain't no fucking Gorillas in Southeast Asia. It's probably just a big monkey".

The Point Man replied, "No sir, it was bigger than a monkey!"

The Lieutenant said to hold up. We hoped that whatever it was would go away. About five minutes later, the Lieutenant gestured to the Point Man to go back out in the jungle and check it out. Two of my Platoon members crouched down and had their weapons pointed in the direction where the Point Man disappeared into the bush.

Soon after the Point Man left, we heard three shots fired in rapid succession. Then our Point Man returned air express, compliments of the so-called Gorilla. We all looked at each other and wondered, "What the fuck?"

At that point, I had to go medically attend the flying soldier. He was semi-conscious and covered with bruises. His fatigues were shredded. I said to him, "I know you are not alright", as I pulled bandages from my bag and stopped the bleeding from his left wrist. I asked him, "What the fuck happened?"

He said, "That thing just beat the piss out of me".

I felt so sorry for him, but still had to laugh. The others went after it and realized that it was either an Orangutan or a large Baboon. The closer they got to it, the angrier it got. When they retreated, it seemed to calm down. It was definitely his territory. We not only had to worry about the NVA Outpost, possible Viet Cong in the area, an injured soldier to take care of, but we also had to contend with a pissed off monkey.

Fortunately, we could establish a clearing near by as a Landing Zone. The Lieutenant called for a Dustoff (Medevac). When the call came back as to the reason for the Dustoff (Medevac), everyone in my Platoon looked at each other. The radiotelephone operator replied,

"He was beat up by a large monkey of unknown origin. Possible multiple fractures of the legs, arms, and possible fracture of the skull. Hurry up, he's hurting bad".

Command approved the request, and the Medevac Helicopter was on its way. I stabilized the victim of the monkey attack. A short time later, the Medevac Helicopter airlifted him out.

The three shots fired during the initial monkey beating was enough cause for us to relocate to a different area of operations, out of fear of alerting the enemy to our position.

While we were waiting for extraction, I thought, "If we go to our west, we will be attacked by wild animals. If we go to our north, we will confront the North Vietnamese Army. If we go south, we will run into the Viet Cong. If we go east, the only thing there is the ocean (South China Sea) and it's shark infested. As Mr. Rogers would say, "It's a beautiful day in the neighborhood".

# The Montagnard Baby

Trying to find the NVA/VC was virtually impossible at times. They made under ground structures and had the ability to hide at a moment's notice. This made the enemy very difficult to locate.

We were somewhere in the Tiger Mountains, exact location unknown. We hacked and cut our way through jungle rather than travel the heavily booby-trapped paths that the NVA/Viet Cong had fixed up for us. The trail that we made led up into the heavily treed mountains.

After about six hours, shear exhaustion set in on all of us. The Lieutenant let us take a break. We freshened up with what little water we had in our canteens. Some soldiers ate while I attended to complaints of soreness and other medical problems from other Platoon members.

After everyone rested, we headed back on our way up the mountain. The mountain did not seem that treacherous, but the thought of the enemy's presence was always on our minds. We knew they were hiding out there in the jungle somewhere.

About an hour later, I thought I spotted something in the jungle to my right. I held up my left hand and made a fist, which told my Platoon to stop. They wondered what was the problem. I pointed to my eyes and pointed in the direction of the movement that I thought I saw. The one Sergeant came over to me and asked, "Doc, what's wrong?"

I replied, "I'm sure I saw something. I have a deep feeling inside that someone is watching us". My Platoon looked all around for a few minutes and everything seemed to be okay.

Still inside, I knew something was about to go wrong. I said, to Lieutenant Ed, "Maybe it's just my imagination".

The Lieutenant asked me what I saw. I replied, "You may think I'm crazy, but I think I just saw a Cannibal".

He laughed and said, "Have you been smoking that funny stuff today? This is Vietnam, not Africa".

After the Point Man checked things out and everything seemed to be good, we continued on our journey. Five minutes later, our Point Man held his fist up for us to stop. Everyone dropped to one knee and was ready to do battle.

The Point Man who is usually 25-30 feet in front of the Platoon, is now back talking to the Lieutenant. I heard him say, "You're not going to believe this, but I think the Ubangis are up there. I think I saw a tribe of them go past me in a flash. They had spears and crossbows".

I thought to myself, "What the hell kind of a place is this?" While The Lieutenant thought for a second then said, "My God, it's probably Montagnards".

(The Central Highlands of Vietnam is the ancestral homeland of a minority called the Montagnard Tribes. Though they are a peace loving people, many of the Montagnards fought with U.S. troops, including the Special Forces, during the Vietnam conflict. Their forests and lands were a battlefield for the Communist desire to rule and the powers that opposed them.)

*Montagnard carved crossbow with three 10-¼ inch long arrows. The crossbow measures 18 inches wide and 13 inches long.*

We continued on our march with more caution. The next thing, we found ourselves surrounded by Montagnard warriors. Some of them held spears and blowguns. Others held miniature cross bows. The weapons appeared to be hand made and very old.

I thought to myself, "It's not bad enough we have the heat, the rain, the jungle, the Viet Cong, the booby traps, and every disease known to mankind to contend with, now we're surrounded by the natives. What the hell could they possibly want?"

They approached us cautiously, but in somewhat of a friendly manner, and appeared not to pose a threat to any of us. The Lieutenant said to everyone, "Do not shoot any body. I repeat, do not shoot. These people are friendly".

The soldier in front of me asked, "If they're so friendly, why are they wearing fuckin' war paint?" Some of the Montagnards had their faces painted with two white strips across their cheeks and one across their forehead. It was enough to put the fear of God in all of us.

As they moved slowly towards us, the leader smiled. All you could see was his black teeth from chewing beetle nut. He had a distinct smell, kind of like last week's garbage. We lowered our weapons. The Montagnards maintained visual contact with all of us. They were a kind of people we never saw before. I knew everyone experienced a large adrenalin rush because of the situation.

One of the tribesman (he looked like the head honcho) put out his hand to shake hands with the Lieutenant. He kept saying, "Bac-si, Bac-si!" It means

Doctor in their dialect. The Lieutenant turned around, pointed to me, and said, "Hey Zoo, I think they want you. Come on up here to the front".

The leader, who we learned later, was the Chief of this group, wanted me to come with him in a most urgent way. He kept smiling and saying, "Bac-si, Bac-si" and held his arms in a cradle position to simulate holding a baby.

The Lieutenant said, "I think they want us to come with them".

They led and we followed them onto a safe trail. The Montagnards knew all of the trails that were free of booby traps. Soon, a small village appeared from underneath the jungle canopy. The population was about 20 to 30 people. When we arrived, we did not know what to expect, or what they wanted with us.

The Chief pointed to me and said, "Bac-si, em la da". This meant, "Doctor, you come". I followed the Chief.

I warned the other men to stick close to me. He led me to the far end of the village. Small children, chickens and older women with big smiles on their faces, chewing beetle nut, greeted me. I now knew why their teeth were black; also, the beetle nut is a mild sedative. I thought to myself, "Now I know why these people seem so happy".

A mamason offered me some beetle nut, but I declined. As we got to the end of the Village, there was a small hut with a weak fire smoldering outside the door. We entered the hut. Now I could understand why they needed a Medic.

There was a young woman in labor in the hut. She was the Chief's daughter. She seemed to be in excruciating pain. I tried to make her feel at ease and reassured her that everything would be okay. I timed her contractions. I found her fully dilated when I examined her. I got my medical bag out and asked someone to get some warm water. I set up my surgical kit.

The Lieutenant said to me, "Hey, Zoo, did you ever deliver a baby before?" I looked at him and said, "I only helped out in the Aid Station once". From reading and observing other births, I felt I knew what to do, however.

At first, I thought this would be an easy birth. Then I discovered the baby's arm and leg tucked up behind his head. It was a breach birth. I knew I was in trouble. I only assisted at one birth, before. It was uneventful and everything happened as nature planned. This became a completely different ball game. After a moment of sheer panic, I regained my composure and returned to the difficult birth.

The Lieutenant interrupted my concentration by inquiring. "What's going on, Zoo? Do you need some help?"

You could cut the tension in my voice with a sword as I replied. "We have a problem. This is going to be a breach birth. I never did one before. I'm a little bit nervous, but I think I can handle it".

The Lieutenant suggested we get a Medevac Helicopter in and have her taken back to Company B Medical. I told him, "By the time the Helicopter gets here the baby will be born. Call it in anyway, because both the mother and baby might have to go back to Company B Medical".

The rest of the Platoon secured the village. Last thing we needed was a firefight during the delivery. I managed to get my hands positioned and moved the baby back up into the birth canal. The woman was screaming with pain. There were about five Native women putting cool rags on her face and talking to her in the Montagnard dialect.

With the Lieutenant, the Chief, and the women in the hut, it was very crowded and hot. I was sweating like a Polar Fox on Miami Beach in mid summer.

I felt around and gently moved the baby's leg from against his ear and repositioned it to a normal birth position.

The woman was crying out in agony, and bleeding heavily. I did not want to risk giving her morphine because it would lower her blood pressure. The baby started coming and I had to have a Platoon member hold the baby's head as it was partially out of the birth canal. Then, I started an IV, of normal saline solution, to adjust for the blood loss. Once the IV was finished, I went back to the birth.

The baby's leg and arm were now in good position for a safe birth. The baby had no further problem being born. I clamped the
Umbilical cord with hemostats and cut it free from the mother. I gave the baby a slight tap on the rear and she began to cry. It was a girl!

At that point, the rest of the Village women took over and I went outside with the Lieutenant and the Chief of this village. The new grandfather had a great big smile on his face. I looked at my Platoon members and cried with relief as I wiped the sweat from my face.

The Medevac arrived a few minutes later and flew the baby and mother back to Company B Medical in case of complications.

A few minutes later, the Chief decided he was going to celebrate the new birth. He broke out jugs of Rice Wine and assorted food native to the jungle (which would also make a Billy Goat vomit).

The pressure seemed to be off everyone. Within the hour, our Platoon was on its way from the Village back into the jungle. Before we left, the Chief came to me and said, "Bac-si number one". He handed me a solid gold bracelet.

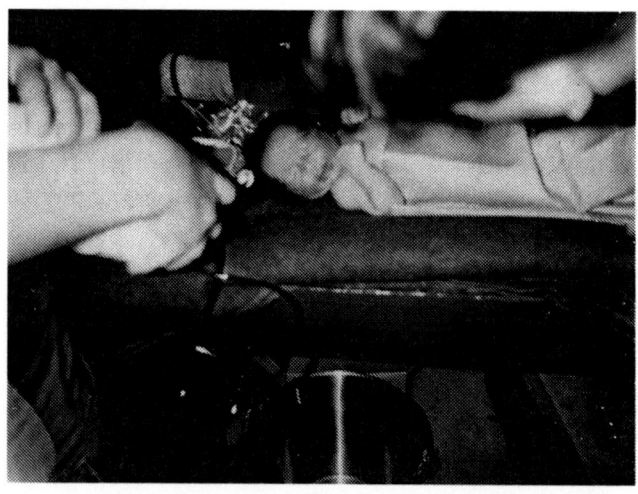

*Doc Zoo in the Tiger Mountains delivered Montagnard baby. She is on a Medevac and on her way to CO B Medical Aid Station.*

The rest of the afternoon wore on as we continued our trek through the jungle looking for NVA/Viet Cong soldiers. I thanked God for letting me do the right things in the Montagnard Village at a very tense and strenuous moment. I felt grateful that the mother and baby survived the birth ordeal and wondered what would happen to all of us if I failed and the outcome was not as rosy.

# VC or VD

If the Viet Cong do not kill you, the venereal diseases that the women carried, will. There were all sorts of venereal diseases infecting our troops. Some cases were so bad that they were incurable and soldiers were dying because of it.

It seemed every time that my Platoon was back in the field after a stand down, at least four or five men would come to me with crotch itch or some other problem as a result of their trip into Bong Song to visit prostitutes.

A rumor circulated that the North Vietnamese were engaging in biological warfare. Supposedly, they had a deadly disease, called Black Syphilis, with which they infected prostitutes. They figured it was a good way to get rid of the 173$^{rd}$ Airborne.

Before every stand down (break from the jungle), I told my Platoon members, "If you're going anywhere where you will have sexual contact with a lady please use protection. It is available through me or you can pick it up at the Aid Station before you leave for town".

The soldiers went to the Aid Station for condoms. They used the rubbers, however, to put over the barrels of their M-16 to keep out water and dirt.

Every so often, the Brass ordered me to make a trip into Bong Song to visit with the village prostitutes and treat them for venereal disease, as needed.

Staff Sergeant Ray arrived at the tail end of my speech to my Platoon. He said, "There's the sorry mother fucker now". He looked right at me and continued. "Hey Zoo, I got enough supplies so you can treat all of the women while you are in Bong Song".

When I arrived in Bong Song on my medical mission, all of the girls would always ask me, "Bac-si want boom-boom (sex)?"

I always said, "No, thanks!"

If I saw symptoms that I thought were unusual I would have a MP escort the woman to the aid station so a doctor could further evaluate her and determine a course of treatment. It is a hellish way to earn a Civil Action Medal.

The preaching and the concern about gonorrhea were necessary. If a soldier caught the disease, it could result in his punishment by an Article 15 (Uniform Code of Military Justice, Non judicial Punishment, refers to certain limited punishments, which can be awarded for minor disciplinary offenses, by a Commanding Officer).

So, one day here I come, the Medic, and I think I have the clap. My symptoms seemed to match those of the clap. I was hurting so I went to the doctor on call at the Aid Station. He said I had prostatitis. It comes from either too much or not enough sex. In my case, it was not enough. He cured me the hard way, by putting pressure on my Prostate and forcing me to ejaculate. At least, I felt better after that experience.

After months and months of my lecturing, it seems that it finally sank into the minds of my Platoon, at least, to use protection when going to town.

# THE WANTED POSTER
# AND THE SPIDER

As the days went on, it seemed to get hotter and hotter in the jungle. We endured our usual ritual of looking for the enemy, but not finding him. This is when Command decided to break the Platoons down into five man Platoons called "Killer Platoons/Hawk".

One such Platoon was coming into Fire Base Solis. One of the soldiers, named Ed, tripped on a piece of barbed wire while entering the perimeter of the Base. He severely cut his knee. At that time, I was out of antibiotics, but I knew he was in pain. I attended to his wound by pouring alcohol on it to keep it from becoming infected. Then I bandaged his knee. He received additional treatment at Company B Medical.

The "Hawk" Platoons would go day and night. When we did encounter some enemy action, it was usually small. It seemed that we beat the enemy or they just wanted to stay away from us.

We went over the same locations time after time. It became frustrating because we knew the enemy was near us, but for some reason we could not engage them. One day our Point Man yelled, "Hold up". Everybody got down to one knee waiting for action.

Then the Point Man came back holding up a piece of paper in his hand and handed it to Lieutenant Ed. He looked at it for a minute and then showed it to all of us. It turned out to be a wanted poster "dead or alive" for any member of the 173rd Airborne Brigade.

*Wanted Poster circulated by the NVA for any 173rd Airborne Soldier.*

The poster was a thrilling thing to see. It made us all want to pick up the pace. Any of us taken alive was not an option. The bond between us was too strong to be broken and each one of us would fight to the death to save the other.

A few days went by without seeing the enemy. Everyone's guard seemed to be getting lax. We stopped to take a brief break in a secure area of the jungle. As we sat and rested, Mike and I heard a noise.

The bushes started to move and we both immediately had our guns pointed right at the disturbance. Suddenly an NVA Soldier's head popped through the bush. He was looking around but did not see our Squad sitting right there. How he missed seeing us is beyond me, as I was almost in his face as he peered through the bush.

The NVA Soldier confidently retracted his head from the shrub and then disappeared. We were all up, armed and ready to fight. We looked around the area and realized that the NVA Soldier was the Point Man and the rest of his Platoon was behind him.

We quick got ready for an ambush. Soon after, ten NVA Soldiers walked right into our trap. The claymore mines that we hid on their path made short work of destroying the enemy. Our Squad did not have any casualties. We knew the NVA would normally come back to recover their dead, so we went through the enemy's belongings. I picked up a nice hammock that was lying on the ground.

I thought to myself, "I could use this instead of laying on the cold ground at night".

As we moved to a different location, I kept thinking about the new hammock that I just acquired. I could not wait to try it out. Then I began wondering if my 6'3" frame would fit into it.

After about four more hours of searching for the enemy with no success, we set up camp for the night. As usual, I had last guard duty and I did not go out on night ambush. (Night ambush included five men, "Kill Platoons" or "Hawk Platoons". They go out, set claymore mines, and trip flares. They also act as a decoy to protect the camp.)

I looked forward to getting some rest as I unfolded the captured NVA hammock. There was a big bloodstain in the middle of it. After I set it up and tied it between two trees, I washed the blood off the canvas with alcohol that I had in my Aid Bag. It was a little creepy and I became a little leery about getting in the hammock, knowing someone else's blood was already on it. I finally decided that it looked too comfortable to pass up, so I decided to try it out.

When I got in it, I found it to be wide enough and it was about eight feet long. I hung my feet out of it to sleep. It sure beat sleeping on the ground.

That day I seemed to be more tired than usual and it was still light when I found myself dozing off in the hammock. Just as I was just starting to feel comfortable, I felt something moving around by my groin. I did not pay too much attention at first because I was so damn tired. Then I felt it starting to crawl up towards my stomach and chest area.

At first, I thought it might be a Bamboo Viper. When I slowly opened my eyes, I almost shit! The thing was right on my chest. It was a large spider, black, and silver, about the size of a can of Spam. It looked like it must have weighed about four pounds.

It had big, furry legs. I looked at it and thought to myself, "Oh, my, now what?" I did not know what to do. I did not know if it was venomous. It suddenly stopped crawling up my chest and seemed to be looking at me.

*A Tarantula crawled on Zoo while he tried to nap in the captured hammock.*

With one quick jab, I punched the spider in the face with my right hand. It flew off my chest. The rolling motion that I started with the punch continued as the hammock turned over and dumped me on my face, on the ground.

Unfortunately, my legs did not come with me. They were in a hammerlock, stuck in the hammock. Being upside down, with my face on the ground and my legs stuck in the hammock made me feel like one of those circus acrobats that hang from the big top by their ankles.

I could see the spider, on the ground now, in some sort of attack mode. It made, what sounded like a war cry, and reared up on its hind legs.

It looked like two fangs protruded from the Spider's mouth. I tried to reach for my pistol while pleading for someone to help me. Doug came up to my rescue and rifle butted the big spider. The spider screamed and then died. I finally freed my legs from the hammock and slept the rest of the night on the ground.

Mike said that he was the one who ended up in possession of the hammock after the spider incident.

# The Hoa Tans

We were pulling operations at the base of the Tiger Mountains by setting up ambush sights and demolitions in and around the Hoa Tan Villages.

*Zoo sets demo charge to blow up NVA hideout in Tiger Mountains.*

The settlements consisted of separate villages; all named Hoa Tan and numbered one through seven.

Hoa Tan 2 was the largest of the villages and definitely the most dangerous. It seemed that anytime we got near any of these villages there was always a confrontation with the NVA/Viet Cong. Delta Company planned to make an amphibious assault at Lo Dieu Beaches. The 3rd Platoon ran interference for them.

Hoa Tan 2 was like an obstacle course around booby traps. The traps consisted of rows of punji stakes sticking out of the ground at an angle. There were also punji stake pits and land mines. As we approached the out skirts of Hoa Tan 2, a small hut located by a stream seemed to be harboring some NVA.

Approximately 200 yards out from the village we started to receive small arms fire from the village. A bullet got our Point Man, Reb. We immediately started to lay down evasive fire.

When I got to Reb, I found he had a deep flesh wound across his arm. As I took care of his arm, the fighting became more aggressive and it was definitely to our favor. We fought our way into the village itself. There were innocent villagers mixed in with the enemy and it became confusing to know who to shoot and who not to shoot. After going door-to-door and searching everywhere for escape tunnels, a U.S. Helicopter flew overhead with an Officer screaming through a bullhorn, "Do not fire on this village. They are innocent people".

*Air assault into the Hoa Tan Villages.*

The NVA/Viet Cong disappeared. The fighting stopped but we continued our search for the enemy. The villagers acted as if they never saw the NVA/Viet Cong and were innocent of any crimes. After a search, we found nothing. We rounded up a few suspicious looking people that we wanted to interrogate. It continued to be very confusing for most of us because we still could not tell the enemy from the villagers.

Later, we moved to a different area at the base of the Tiger Mountains. I just finished with sick call. Lieutenant Ed said to me, "Zoo, when you are finished I want to talk to you".

When I finished sick call, I could not help wondering if there was anything wrong with my performance. When I got to Lieutenant Ed, he was reading a map. I said, "Yes sir, what can I do for you?"

He looked up, smiled at me, and shook my hand. He said, "Good job, Doc. I am gonna miss you. You have ten minutes to say your good-byes to everyone. You're going back to LZ Uplift".

At first I looked at him and asked, "Like, why?"

He said, "You tour of duty is up. Besides, you have been in Vietnam way too long. Let someone else fight the war".

I was torn between wanting to finally go home yet leaving the Platoon of soldiers with whom I enjoyed such camaraderie. I went around to each and everyone of my Platoon. I shook their hands and gave each of them a hug. We vowed one day to meet again.

As I waited in a small, secured perimeter I could hear the Chopper coming. I heard the sound of the pop smoke for the last time, telling the Pilot that it was safe to come in. The Helicopter hovered and then slowly came down over the Landing Zone that my Platoon had set up.

I scrambled to the Helicopter and waited for the new Medic to exit the aircraft. He hopped off the Chopper with a huge rucksack. It reminded me of my first days in the jungle with my overweight rucksack. I shook his hand and said, "Take care of my boys. Good luck, you're going to need it".

I chuckled as the Crew Chief helped me aboard while I watched the new Medic struggle to walk with his heavy rucksack.

As we were taking off, I sat in the doorway of the Helicopter with my feet on the skids. I gave everyone the Peace sign as we slowly flew away from the perimeter and headed to LZ Uplift.

# Shit Burning

After I arrived at LZ Uplift, I tried to decide whether to make the Army a career or go back to college. While back at the LZ, before I headed to the States, I still did my duties in the Aid Station, which included working on casualties and pulling sick call.

There was one particular duty that no body at the Aid Station liked or wanted to do. Sanitary reasons, made the job necessary, however. The first couple of times I performed this duty, breakfast became unappealing. It was a very nasty job. Everyone had to take his turn at this duty, however.

This was "shit burning" duty. The camp had a large outhouse with about ten stalls. Instead of the urine and feces going into the ground and into a lime base, it fell into a cut in half fifty-five gallon drum.

There was one under every toilet seat. The drums had handles made by cutting a metal flap on the side of the barrel with a torch. This also made it easier to pick up the barrels.

Inside of the drum, there was a mixture of kerosene and gasoline. This mixture absorbed the excrement and toilet paper. After a day or two, when the barrels became semi full, the "shit burner" removed them and replaced them with fresh drums.

Once removed from the toilets, the drums are set a safe distance away from the latrine. The "shit burner" then lights the drums simultaneously. As the excrements burned away, the shit burner had to go to each barrel and stir it with a long stick.

*A soldier performs "shit burning" duty.*

It was one of my last days in Vietnam. Of course, Command sees fit to assign me to the "shit burning" detail. I was in a big hurry to get it done, so I could go to the Commissary to get a few last things before leaving.

I just put a sign up that the latrines were closed for five minutes while I changed the barrels. Then I noticed someone coming from the Aid Station and walking towards the latrine. I did not know him, but I asked him if he could wait a minute while I changed the barrels. He looked at me with a pissed off appearance on his face and mumbled something under his breath that I did not understand.

At this point, I heard him go into the latrine at the place where I was changing the barrels. He plopped his ass on the toilet seat.

I was outside looking up at his ass and said to him, "I asked you to wait a minute, didn't I?"

His reply was, "Aw go fuck yourself".

It really pissed me off when he told me to go fuck myself. As I slid the barrel under his toilet he let loose and his shit hit my shirt, my face, splashed into the fresh kerosene which in turn splashed all over me. I thought to myself, "You rotten, fuckin', prick. I'll fix your ass".

I picked up one of the wooden shit stirrers, dipped it in kerosene and gasoline, and ignited it. Then I stuck the insolent soldier right in the ass with it. I know I singed some of the hair off his ass because he let out a scream. He yelled to me, "When I get out of here, I'm going to kick your fucking ass".

That is all I needed get me going. I closed the trap door on his stall and walked around to the front where his stall door was. I stood by the door and I listened for him to unhook the latch.

Before he could open the door, I ripped the door open, pulled him out by his throat, punched him in the mouth, pushed him back into the stall, grabbed him and put him upside down. Then I put his head in the toilet. I asked him, "How do you like the view, now?"

Some Soldiers had to carry him to the Aid Station. They had to put cream on his burnt ass. He possibly had a broken nose and a slight concussion.

Staff Sergeant Ray came out of the Aid Station yelling, "You sorry mother fucker, you broke his jaw and nose and burnt his asshole off. You done stepped on your dick this time, Zoo".

I explained to the Sergeant why I took the action. I told him I was very sorry. He chuckled and said, "The guy was a trouble maker anyway. He caused the other Medics some grief and probably deserved what he got".

That evening, at 1700 hours (5:00 PM) we had a short formation outside of the Aid Station. That is where the Sergeant reads the duty roster and daily occurrences. Right before he dismissed everyone, he called me out in front of the other Medics. He awarded me the Good Conduct Medal! Then he sent me home.

Years later, Mike told me, "You got fucked. Sergeants don't burn shit!"

*I went to Cam Rahn Bay, where I boarded a plane headed for the States. It all seemed to happen so quickly. The first thing, I am in the jungle and the next thing I know, I am on a plane going home.*

I knew my parents were going to be very happy to see me and would be waiting to meet my plane when it landed.

For some years after the war, I did not see any of the men I served with until 1998 when we met again at a 173rd Airborne Reunion at Fort Bragg. We renewed our friendship and have been close friends ever since

*Going home, at last. Cam Rahn Bay, September 1970.*

After years of sitting and thinking about that treacherous, dangerous jungle that we lived in, how we ever survived is beyond any reasonable point of thought. The jungle that the 173rd Airborne Brigade lived, fought, and died in would make Jurassic Park seem like a kid's petting zoo.

# Airborne All The Way
# (The Herd)

Sgt. Robert Wayne Costigan ("Doc Zoo")
Company B
Medical, Dustoff, Aid Station and Pharmacy
Company A 1/503rd Airborne Infantry 2nd and 3rd Platoon
173rd Airborne Brigade
Served 1968, 1969, and 1970

## FOR RICHARD
By Helen A. Cummings

2nd Lieutenant, Richard M. Cummings was killed in combat, January 13, 1967 at Tinh Hau Nghia, Vietnam. Awarded Bronze Star with "V" Device; Purple Heart; National Order Medal; Fifth Class and The Gallantry Cross-with Palm, Republic of Vietnam.

*The voice of thy brother's blood crieth unto me from the ground.*
*Genesis 4:10*

*bullet riddled, ambush guns, jungle TET,*
*brother hero, escort home, honor guard,*
*folded flag, wife grieving, funeral shroud,*
*purple heart, bronze star, V for valor,*
*father's sorrow, pride, and tears grow old with him,*
*mother's love, endures a timeless wound,*
*brothers and sisters mourn their mentor lost,*
*a pastel portrait lives his memory now,*
*and grown men are still not ashamed,*
*to send the children to war.*

# WHY?
## By Robert W. Costigan
## Combat Medic Vietnam –'68,'69,'70 with 173rd Airborne Brigade

*Looking into the sun, I cry.*
*a taste of hate fills my mind,*
*and the question remains the same.*

*Each second that passes by,*
*the sun no longer shines,*
*and out of darkness, I ask why?*

*The heartbeat of a wild horse is inside me now,*
*and just like the wind, I must run.*
*Good luck, a voice keeps saying, while inside, my heart*
*keeps praying!*

*Am I to live or to die?*
*It doesn't really matter,*
*With one last look into the open, I'm on my way.*
*Life, just like time, is mine to save!*

*Hands covered with blood, I repair a man as red ants bite my neck. Looking into his eyes, I read his mind. That tells the story so well, of all his dreams he left behind.*

*Time is getting shorter, I must move on. I'll be back shortly, so just hang on, and from a face filled with pain comes a smile and a whisper of "thanks".*

*Again I move, out of fear, I cannot say! Blinded by my own sweat, I make my way. "Take it easy, Soldier, you're OK". Just wish I could tell myself that! And as my hands cover with blood once again, I keep telling myself "Hurry". Suddenly, everything turns cold and dark. Sitting back, I cover his head and just ask why? And wonder whose turn is it next to die?*
*And the red ants are still biting at my neck, my eyes, still blinded by my own sweat, and my question still remains the same,*

*WHY?*

Printed in the United States
206308BV00001B/32/A